# BOOK OF MISTAIKES

Also available from Futura:

THE BOOK OF HEROIC FAILURES
THE BOOK OF INSULTS
THE ENCYCLOPAEDIA OF INSULTING BEHAVIOUR
THE IRISH KAMA SUTRA
THE HENRY ROOT LETTERS
THE BOOK OF EROTIC FAILURES
THE BOOK OF EXCUSES
HEROIC HOAXES
CRITICS' GAFFES

Gyles Brandreth

# Book of Mistaikes

Futura

A Futura Book

First published in Great Britain on behalf of
the Papermate Division of Gillette UK Limited by
Queen Anne Press, a division of Macdonald & Co
(Publishers) Ltd

First Futura edition 1982
Reprinted 1982, 1984, 1986

ISBN 0 7088 2194 4

Illustrations by Graham Thompson

Printed in Great Britain by
Hazell Watson & Viney Limited,
Member of the BPCC Group,
Aylesbury, Bucks

Futura Publications
A Division of
Macdonald & Co (Publishers) Ltd
Greater London House
Hampstead Road
London NW1 7QX
A BPCC plc Company

# CONTENTS

| A | All's Well that Ends Well | 7 |
|---|---|---|
| B | Blunders and Bloomers | 12 |
| C | Calamities with Class | 17 |
| D | Death Where is Thy Sting? | 21 |
| E | English Spoken Here | 27 |
| F | Fantastic Fallacies | 33 |
| G | Goldwynisms | 40 |
| H | Hitting The Headlines | 43 |
| I | It Pays to Advertise | 49 |
| J | Jenuine Mistakes | 57 |
| K | Kinquering Kongs | 63 |
| L | Literary Lapses | 65 |
| M | Magnificent Misprints | 70 |
| N | Not Quite Nice | 79 |
| O | Office Errors | 84 |
| P | Prize Pupils | 89 |
| Q | Quick March | 98 |
| R | Recipes for Disaster | 102 |
| S | Signs of the Times | 106 |
| T | Translation Please | 109 |
| U | Unholy Writ | 115 |
| V | Variety and Spice | 119 |
| W | Window Dressing | 123 |
| X | Xplain Yourself | 129 |
| Y | You Said *What*? | 132 |
| ZZizz | Iz ze end | 135 |

# ALL'S WELL THAT ENDS WELL

**'Man is the only animal that blushes ... or needs to.'**
*Mark Twain* (1835-1910)

Mrs Beverly Nina Avery, from Los Angeles, California, has been divorced sixteen times ... the Decca recording company said 'No' to the Beatles because they thought they were old-fashioned ... a local council demolition team razed a two-storey house to the ground and then discovered it was the wrong one ... *The Daily Telegraph* recently ran a headline that read 'Magistrates Act to keep Theatres Open' ... and not long ago I came across this inscription on a tombstone:

> Sacred to the memory of
> **MAJOR JAMES BRUSH**
> who was killed by
> the
> accidental discharge
> of a pistol by
> his orderly
> 14th of April 1831
> Well done thou good and
> faithful servant

Like it or not, believe it or not, we all make mistakes. Indeed, mistake-making is one of the very few factors that can honestly be said to unite mankind – and this book is intended as a modest tribute to the errors of all our ways.

It is a book packed with mistakes of all kinds – most of them deliberate, of course. However, if one or two unintentional errors have crept in by mistake, I hope you won't overlook them. As an author prone to making mistakes, I'm in excellent company. There have been not-so-deliberate slips in some of the greatest masterpieces of world literature. For example, in Daniel Defoe's novel *Robinson Crusoe*, the ship-wrecked hero decides to salvage some goods from his ship before she disappears completely. Defoe describes how Crusoe removes all his clothes before swimming to the ship, but forgetting this fact he allows him to fill his *pockets* with biscuits once he is on board! And Sir Arthur Conan Doyle gave the immortal Dr Watson one war wound – but in two places. In *A Study in Scarlet* the wound is in the shoulder, while in *The Sign of Four* it is in Watson's leg.

Before you embark on this amazing mystery tour of mishaps, misprints and mistakes of every kind, you'll want to assess your own capacity for spotting unlikely errors, so here's a quick quiz to help you.

1. Copy down the following: A bird in
   in the hand is worth two in the bush.

2. Which is correct? Nine and five *are* thirteen **or** nine and five *is* thirteen?

3. Can you spot any mistakes in these famous quotations?
   a) When Winter comes, is Spring not far behind?
   b) It is a far far better thing I do, than I have ever done.
   c) Alas, poor Yorick. I knew him well.
   d) Oh to be in England now that Spring is here.
   e) On to fresh Fields and Pastures new.
   f) Of the making of books there is no end.
   g) 'Beauty is truth, truth beauty', – that is all
      Ye know on earth, and all ye need to know.

4. Punctuate the following passage as the author might have done.

   Blest if she aint in a queer condition said Mr

Cruncher more and more disturbed Wot can she have been a takin to keep her courage up Hark Theres the roll of them dreadful carts You can hear that miss

I can hear said Miss Pross seeing that he spoke to her nothing O my good man there was a great crash and then a great stillness and that stillness seems to be fixed and unchangeable never to be broken as long as my life lasts

If she dont hear the roll of those dreadful carts now very nigh their journeys end said Mr Cruncher glancing over his shoulder its my opinion that indeed she will never hear anything else in the world

And indeed she never did

5. If red houses are made out of red bricks and yellow houses are made out of yellow bricks, what are green houses made out of?

6. If on the last day of February 1980 – and remember it was a leap year – you had gone to bed at seven o'clock, having set the alarm to wake you at 8.15am how much sleep would you have got?

7. An archaeologist recently claimed that he had found a coin dated 46 BC. Do you think he did?

8. What is it that occurs four times in every week, twice in every month, but only once in a year?

9. A magazine recently attributed the following quotations to the wrong person. Can you tell who originally said each one?
   a) 'The majority is always wrong. The minority is rarely right.'                    *Shirley Williams*

   b) 'Imagination is more important than knowledge.'
                                                    *Arthur Mullard*

   c) 'Genius is one per cent inspiration and ninety-nine per cent perspiration.' *William Shakespeare*

10. Their are five mistaikes in this sentance. Can you spot them?

# SOLUTIONS

1. If you copied the proverb down correctly you should have made the mistake of including the 'in' twice in succession.

2. Neither are correct: nine and five equal fourteen!

3. a) *If* Winter comes, *can* Spring be far behind?
   b) It is a far far better thing *that* I do...
   c) Alas! Poor Yorick. I knew him, Horatio.
   d) ... now that *April's there*.
   e) *Tomorrow* to fresh *Woods* and Pastures new
   f) Of making *many* books there is no end
   g) There is no mistake!

4. The correct punctuation is as follows:
   'Blest if she ain't in a queer condition!' said Mr Cruncher, more and more disturbed. 'Wot can she have been a takin', to keep her courage up? Hark! There's the roll of them dreadful carts! You can hear that, miss?'

   'I can hear,' said Miss Pross, seeing that he spoke to her, 'nothing. O, my good man, there was a great crash, and then a great stillness, and that stillness seems to be fixed and unchangeable, never to be broken as long as my life lasts.'

   'If she don't hear the roll of those dreadful carts, now very nigh their journey's end,' said Mr Cruncher, glancing over his shoulder, 'it's my opinion that indeed she never will hear anything else in this world.'

   And indeed she never did.

5. Green houses are made out of glass!

6. Assuming you do not have a twenty-four hour alarm clock, you will get just 1½ hours rest before the alarm goes off.

7. In 46 BC they would have had no idea that Christ was to be born and so it is impossible to find a coin with that date on it.

8. The letter 'e' – <u>e</u> v <u>e</u> r y w <u>e</u> <u>e</u> k  etc, etc.
                1   2       3 4

9. a) Henrik Ibsen
   b) Albert Einstein
   c) Thomas Alva Edison

10. The mistakes are:
    a) 'Their' instead of 'there'
    b) 'Mistaikes' instead of 'mistakes'
    c) 'Sentance' instead of 'sentence'
    d) The fact that there are four mistakes, not five!

# BLUNDERS AND BLOOMERS

This chapter is dedicated to one Peter Balfour, a Scottish businessman, who met the Prince of Wales at a public reception shortly after the announcement of Prince Charles's engagement to Lady Diana Spencer. Mr Balfour, being a loyal and gallant gentleman, invited the assembled company to raise their glasses and join him in a toast to the lifelong happiness of 'Prince Charles and Lady Jane'!

Fortunately for us (if unfortunately for Mr Balfour) verbal blunders like this aren't quickly forgotten. Here, culled from newspaper reports, radio and television interviews and memorable conversations, are some of my favourite slips of the tongue – all of them uttered by the unsuspecting and the innocent who found that what they had said wasn't quite what they had intended...

'The bride wore a long white dress that fell to the floor.'

'For those of you who have small children and don't know it we have a *crèche* downstairs.'

★

'Wash your face in the morning and neck at night.'

★

'Mrs Johnson can prepare mashed potatoes as fluffy and delicious as any of my acquaintances.'

★

'Even more astonishing was our saving the lives of little babies who formerly died from sheer ignorance.'

★

'In Germany a person cannot slaughter any animal without being rendered unconscious first.'

★

'The women included their husbands and children in their potluck suppers.'

★

'A gentleman never crumbles his bread or rolls in his soup.'

★

'There was a party for the children and after they were tucked up in bed a lot of fun for the parents.'

★

'I told him to leave my organ alone, but he kept on playing with the knobs.'

★

'The captain was always putting his privates through such terrible exercises.'

★

'If the baby does not thrive on raw milk, boil it.'

★

'So, I leant out of the window in my nightdress...'

★

'If the vicar does get a Sunday free, we like nothing better than to have it off with friends.'

★

'I wish your workmen would come and fill in the hole because we are fed up with having it outside the gate. It

13

is becoming an attraction, and we don't know how to get rid of all the children.'

★

'She is a female woman of the opposite sex.'

★

'I have been under the doctor for three weeks and it's done nothing for my condition.'

★

'The soldier was shot in the Ardoyne area but survived.'

★

'In 1675 Frederick William defeated a Swedish army twice his size.'

★

'Wood doesn't grow on trees you know.'

★

'In England this happens a hundred times out of a hundred – that's nearly always.'

★

'If you wish to talk, ask me first.'

★

'This man is a very efficient machine.'

★

'Watch with one eye and listen with the other.'

★

'In a word – I don't think so.'

★

'She's a man, nothing else.'

★

'I can't blame you for wanting to go outside and sit on your ten minute break.'

★

'The summary of information contains totals of the numbers of students broken down by sex, marital status, and age.'

★

'Will you lend me a rifle so as I can shoot myself?'

★

'We had the Brown family for dinner on Monday
evening.'

'Your head looks just like my husband's behind.'

*

'Just because there are cannibals here there is no need to get into a stew.'

*

'He spent his early life on the back of a horse with a pipe in his mouth.'

*

'The big limitation about "on" is that it is a bit limited.'

*

'They still use inches to measure horses' hands.'

*

'Caesar might have been a bit of an old woman, but he was still a man.'

*

'She let the knife slip and cut herself severely in the pantry.'

*

'This is a compulsory part of the exam, and you have to take it.'

*

'This book was written by the very famous A.J. Herbertson who actually went to the same university as I did in 1894.'

*

'When the water reaches 25°C, take the temperature.'

*

'That's the most illegible excuse I've ever heard.'

*

'I apologise for biting your heads off.'

*

# CALAMITIES WITH CLASS

**'History is indeed little more than the register of the crimes; follies, and misfortunes of mankind.'**
*Edward Gibbon* (1737-94)

To say nothing of his mistakes...

One of the most spectacular military defeats of all time occurred in 1862 during the American Civil War when one General Ambrose Burnside ordered his troops to cross a river by means of a very narrow bridge. Because of the bridge's width, the soldiers could only move across very slowly and no more than two abreast, with the direct result that they became an easy target for the enemy and were all shot.

Had the General been more adroit he would have discovered that the river was only just over two feet deep and the troops could easily have walked through unseen.

Not surprisingly, President Lincoln paid this tribute to Burnside:
'Only he could wring spectacular defeat out of the jaws of victory.'

\*

François de Civille was pronounced dead in 1562 and was duly buried. Six hours after the funeral his brother had an intuition that François was still alive and promptly went along to the cemetery and disinterred him. The 'corpse' revived and lived seventy years longer, dying at the age of 105 as the result of a cold contracted whilst serenading his sweetheart all night long.

\*

In 1818 in Great Yarmouth a boy was baptised as a girl. Two weeks later the mistake was discovered and the child was re-baptised as a boy.

In 1811, for a small wager, a blacksmith in Stroud devoured one pint of periwinkles, complete with shells, in ten minutes. He then repeated the feast on request, and died, unable to learn from his mistake.

*

Two rival Frenchmen fought a duel in 1808, not in the usual way but above the gardens of Tuileries each in a hot air balloon. Instead of firing at each other, they used blunderbusses and aimed at their rival's balloon. At half-a-mile high the men fired, simultaneously hitting the balloons causing them to bite the earth, killing both occupants.

*

The prehistoric monster known as the Iguanodon was much misunderstood when its skeleton was first discovered in the nineteenth century.

Apart from being named after the Iguana (which it in no way resembled), when assembling the skeleton the reconstructors made two fundamental errors. They erected the skeleton with the animal walking on its four legs, and finding an oddly shaped bone left over, took it to be a horn and placed it on the creature's forehead making it appear rather like a unicorn.

It was not until many years had passed that further investigations revealed that the Iguanodon had actually walked on its two hind legs, and the surplus spiked bone was in fact a type of thumb, which should have been attached to the hand.

*

In 1919 during the Peace Conference at Versailles, David Lloyd George came up with the marvellous suggestion that the Italian government could replace the commercial losses they had suffered during World War I by increasing their banana production. In theory it sounded very convincing but there was just one snag ... they don't grow bananas in Italy.

In 1873 the composer Tchaikovsky made his first attempt at writing a piano concerto, and dedicated it to his friend and teacher, Nicholas Rubenstein, who had agreed to play the piano part at its first public performance. On attempting it for the first time, however, Rubenstein subjected the composer to very severe criticism, claiming that the piece was unplayable and unsuited to the piano. Tchaikovsky took great offence at this and removed Rubenstein's name from the title page, substituting that of Hans Von Bulow. Later the piece was played by Bulow, to great acclaim, and the piece which Rubenstein had criticised as unplayable is now regarded as one of the greatest concertos of all time – the *Piano Concerto in B Flat Minor (Opus 23)*.

*

Even if you are not fond of animals, never make the mistake of being unkind to pets. In 1917 a wealthy Austrian woman, Mathilde Kovacs, burned her entire fortune just before her death – because her next of kin had been unfriendly towards her cats and consequently she didn't want her heartless relatives to enjoy any of her fortune.

In September 1944, a Brooklyn lawyer left over £25,000 to his cat, thereby cutting out five relatives 'because of their contemptuous attitude towards the cat', and in 1781 a peasant from Toulouse appointed in his will 'my chestnut horse as sole legatee'.

*

In one of his portraits of Charles I, Anthony Van Dyke painted the king with two gauntlets. Both of them were for the right hand.

*

A century ago Dr Dionysys Lardner of University College, London, claimed that no large steamship would ever be able to cross the Atlantic because it would require more coal than it could possibly carry.

Just two years later the *Great Western* crossed the Atlantic.

*

In 1876 the outlaw, Jesse James, was killed during a gunfight when he and his gang tried to rob a bank. The shooting began when the cashier refused to unlock the safe. Jesse James died not knowing that the safe had actually been open all the time.

*

In English history, one of the greatest mistakes was made by a baker called John Farynor who went to bed one evening leaving one of his baking ovens alight. Sometime during the early hours of 2 September 1666 sparks set fire to the bakery and before long the blaze had spread to neighbouring buildings. Soon more than half of London was aglow.

A steady wind served as bellows to the flames as they spread through the city, destroying houses, shops, warehouses, nearly ninety churches, the entire financial centre of the city, and the great St Paul's Cathedral, where it is said the tombs burst open revealing bodies of those long since dead.

The Great Fire of London is one of the few disasters to be honoured with a permanent reminder – the Monument, which, if it was to fall over in the direction of Pudding Lane, would land on the home of John Farynor, the baker.

# DEATH WHERE IS THY STING?

We live and learn.

Then, of course, we die and forget it all, which is probably no bad thing, given the fatal mis-understandings – not to say grave errors – that can creep on to the inscriptions on our tombstones.

Somebody once said: 'If men could see the epitaphs their friends write they would believe they had got into the wrong grave...'

Somebody else once said: 'An epitaph is a statement that usually lies above about the one that lies below...'

I say: 'It's no wonder cremation is becoming so popular when you get real grave-stone epitaphs like these...'

'Alice Mary Johnson 1883-1947
Let her RIP.'

*

'Mary Anne has gone to rest
Safe at last on Abraham's breast,
Which may be nuts for Mary Anne,
But it's certainly rough on Abraham.'

*

'Here lies the body of
SAMUEL YOUNG
Who came here and died
for the benefit of his health.'

*

'In loving memory of
SYDNEY WILLIAM SMYTHE
1898-1951
Cherished by his wife.
Rest in Peace – Until we meet again.'

'Here lies in silent clay
Miss Arabella Young
Who on the 21st of May
Began to hold her tongue.'

*

The following inscription was found on the tombstone
of an auctioneer named Knight at Greenwood:

GOOD KNIGHT
GOING
GOING
GONE
1868

*

BIGHAM YOUNG
Born on this spot 1801
A man of courage
and superb equipment.

*

'Here lies the body of JOHN MOUND
Who was lost at sea and never found.'

*

'This gallant young man
gave up his life
in the attempt
to save a perishing lady.'

*

*Epitaph on a dentist*
'Stranger approach this spot with gravity;
John Brown is filling his last cavity.'

*

'Richard Kendrick
was buried here on
August 29th, 1785
by the desire of his wife
Margaret Kendrick.'

*

'Here lies Elizabeth Wise
Who died of thunder sent from Heaven
In 1777.'

★

'Here in this grave, there lies a Cave,
We call a cave a grave.
If cave be grave, and grave be Cave,
Then, reader, judge, I crave,
Whether doth Cave lie here in grave,
Or grave here lie in Cave:
If grave in Cave here buried lie,
Then, grave, where is thy victory?
Go, reader, and report, here lies a Cave,
Who conquers death, and buries his own grave.'

★

'Bless my i, i, i, i, i,
Here he lies,
In a sad Pickle
Kill'd by Icicle.
In the Year of Anno Domini 1776.'

★

'The Lord saw good, I was lopping off wood,
And down fell from the tree;
I met with a check, and I broke my neck,
And so death lopp'd off me!'

★

'Here lies the remains of Thomas Nicolls,
Who died in Philadelphia, March 1578.
Had he lived, he would have been buried here.'

★

'Here lies the body of
SARAH
Wife of John Hayes
who died 24th March 1823AD
aged 42 years
The Lord giveth and the Lord taketh away.
Blessed be the name of the Lord.'

'Here lies I at ye church door,
Here I lie, because I'se poor.
Ye furder you go, ye more you pay,
Here I lie as warm as they.'

★

'Here lies
Father and Mother and Sister and I.
We all died within the space of one short year.
They all be buried at Wimble, except I
And I be buried here.'

★

'My time was come! My days were spent!
I was called – and away I went!!'

★

'Fear God
Keep the commandments
and
Don't attempt to climb a tree
For that's what caused the death of me!'

★

'Here lies the body of
MARY ELLIS
Daughter of Thomas Ellis
and Lydia, his wife, of this parish.
She was a virgin of virtuous character
and most promising hopes.
She died on the third of June 1609
aged one hundred and nineteen.

★

'Erected to the memory of
JOHN PHILIPS
accidently shot
as a mark of affection by
his brother.'

★

'Here lies the body of
THOMAS VERNON
The only surviving son
of
Admiral Vernon
Died 23rd July 1753.'

★

'Misplacing – mistaking –
Misquoting – misdating –
Men, manners, things, facts all,
Here lies Nathan Wraxall.'

★

'Here lies the body of John Eldred,
At least, he will be when he's dead;
But now at this time he is alive,
The 14th August, Sixty-five.'

★

'Here lies the body of Mary Anne Lowder
She burst while drinking a seidlitz powder.
Called from this world to her heavenly rest,
She should have waited till it effervesced.'

★

'Erected to the memory of
JOHN MacFARLANE
Drowned in the waters of Lieth
By a few affectionate friends.'

★

'In memory of
JOHN SMITH
who met weirlent death neer this
spot 18 hundred 40 too.
He was shot by his own pistol.
It was not one of the new kind
but an old fashioned brass barrel,
and of such is the
Kingdom of Heaven.'

★

'Here lies Ann Mann;
She lived an old maid
and died an old Mann.'

★

'In remembrance of
NICHOLAS TOKE
He married five wives whom he survived.
At the age of 93 he walked to London
to seek a sixth but died before he
found her.'

★

'Here lies
JOHN JAMES COOK
who was a faithful servant to his master
and an upright downright honest man
1760.'

★

'Here lies the body of poor Frank Row,
Parish clerk and grave stone cutter.
And this is writ to let you know,
What Frank for others us'd to do
Is now for Frank done by another.'

★

'Grim death took me without any warning,
I was well at night and dead at nine in the
morning.'

★

**Postscript**
*From the Last Will and Testament of David Davis,*
*died 1788*
'I, David Davis, of Clapham, Surrey, do give and
bequeath to Mary David, daughter of Peter Delaport,
the sum of five shillings, which is sufficient to enable
her to get drunk for the last time at my expense.'

# ENGLISH SPOKEN HERE

When the British venture abroad they expect the foreigners they encounter – and they don't like to meet too many of them – to speak English. The British speak English perfectly and, if they can do it, they don't see why the rest of the world shouldn't have a go as well. On the whole the system works adequately (and the British, being a jolly accommodating race, help out by addressing all foreigners as loudly and clearly as possible) which is perhaps surprising since there is no denying the fact that English isn't the simplest of languages to master. So many of the same words and phrases take on totally different connotations depending on the circumstances in which they are used...

'Johnnie', said his mother. 'Will you run across the road and see how old Mrs Jones is this morning, please.'

'Yes, mum!' he shouted, and returned a couple of minutes later with the reply: 'Mrs Jones says it's none of your business how old she is!'

*

Given that very few English people can explain why you can 'water a horse' but you can't 'milk a cat', it is not really to be wondered at that foreigners have such a terrible time when trying to turn their native tongues into English. Recently I met a young Frenchman with a very nasty-looking black eye, the result of a hefty slap around the face from his English ex-girlfriend. He had meant to say to her 'When I look into your eyes, time stands still', but unfortunately he translated this sweet nothing as: 'Your face would stop a clock!'

*

Even trained interpreters can get it wrong. 'Out of sight, out of mind' was translated into Russian and then translated back into English by a Soviet interpreter as

'Invisible lunatic', while the Chinese misinterpreted the slogan 'Come alive with Pepsi' as 'Pepsi brings your relatives back from the dead'.

★

Native English speakers do occasionally have problems with other languages: a Ford motor car was to be called the 'Caliente' until the company discovered the word meant 'streetwalker' in Mexican, and Chevrolet were to name a new model the 'Chevrolet Nova' until they learnt that 'no-va' means 'won't go'. But as a rule, whatever the language, *we* know what we're talking about and *they* don't. As proof positive, here is a selection of quotations from around the world found in establishments that proudly boast 'English spoken here'...

*From a guidebook about Malta*
'Although every care has been taken, us do not accept responsibility for inoccurancies.'

★

*An advertisement in a Belgian forwarding office*
'Hand your baggage to us. We will send it in all directions.'

★

*Instructions in a Madrid lift*
'To move the cabin, push button of wishing floor. If the cabin shuld enter more persons, each-one should press number of wishing floor. Driving is then going alphabetically by natural order. Button retaining pressed position shows received command for visiting station.'

★

*Handbill from the festival in Pamplona, Spain*
'What you must *not* do:

28

To walk around alone or in groups, in an inadequate form and adapting attitudes that denote a personal bad state, to offend the elemental conduct.

To make noises and scandlas in the sight of the public and establishments.

Sit down or lie down in sight of the public, to obstruct the freedom of the people.

Utilizing ponds, fountains, for personal use.

To break or tear objects in the sight of the public or crowded places.

To utilize percussion instruments after midnight.'

*Notice in the foyer of a Japanese hotel*
'Sports jackets may be worn, but no trousers.'

*Notice in a Spanish hotel*
'It is forbidden to steal hotel towels please.
If you are not person to do such is please not to read this
notice.'

*

*Bedroom notice in a Milan hotel*
'Do not adjust your light hanger. If you wish to have it
off the manageress will oblige you.'

*

*Seen over a shop in Jolluner, India*
'Sex Specialist (England Returned)'

*

*From a guidebook about Sardinia*
'To remember of this period are the failed lading of the
French revolutionaries on the northern coast of the
island (1793), the uprising of 1795, the consequent
march of the judge C.M. Angioi on Cagliari, thwarted
off at Oristano in 1796 and the attempt also fruitless of
the notary Cilocca in 1802.'

*

*From a guidebook about Gerona*
'Gerona. Here is a name and a symbol. A name set in
the tentacles of the Empire. Of aristocratic craddle. Old
and fruitful savour, speaking about daring legions,
unfinishing ways, aqueducts, warlike marching and
toges. Gerona was promise and reality. Promise
because upon it would fall the evangelic seed of the
mustard, not because less strong in the aborescence
and the fruit.'

*

*Notice on an Italian camp site*
'By order of the Police, one obliges the frequenters of
the Camping to are wearing bath-costumes that are not
giving offence to the Morals.'

*

*Sign in a Ladies room in a restaurant in India*
'For sanitation purposes please sanit in the pots
provided and not on the floor.'

30

*Notice in an Italian hotel*

'Visitors are requested not to throw coffee or other matter into the basin. Why else it stuffs the place inconvenient for the other world.'

★

*Instructions on a foreign food packet*

'To do what: Besmear a backing-pan, previously buttered with a good tomato sauce and after, dispose Canelloni, lightly distanced between them in a only couch.'

★

*Notice in a village café in France*

'Persons are requested not to occupy seats in this café without consummation.'

★

*Advertisement in a Spanish newspaper*

'English shorthand typist. Efficien. Useless. Apply otherwise.'

★

*Notice in an Austrian hotel*

'In case of fire please do your utmost to alarm hall porter.'

★

*Advertisement in a Brazilian newspaper*

'Paying guest. Goog opporuny for a snigla refined gentleman. Large room nicely furnished, splendidd food. Six sindoros facing sea, quite close to bashing beach.'

★

**Postscript**

The following conversation was heard in England, in an English car, with a typically English driving instructor: 'Now, we are all set to go. To begin with just turn the jigger over and push on the hickey with your left hand and pull down on the other little jim-crack with your right, then press down the doodah with your foot, pull the thingmybob at the same time, and when it starts you

push down on the dooberry with your left foot and yank
the umptydiddy back, then let up the foot on the dingus
and put your other foot on the hickey-madoodle; and
don't forget to push down on the hootnanny everytime
you move the whatyoumaycallit, and you'll be hunky-
dory, see?'

Surprisingly, all the learner driver said was:
'Pardon ...?'

# FANTASTIC FALLACIES

**'Man can believe in the impossible, but man can never believe the improbable.'**
*Oscar Wilde* (1856-1900)

Can you face facts? Can you bear to accept that Cinderella never wore glass slippers, that Lady Godiva never rode naked through the streets of Coventry, that Marie-Antoinette never said 'Let them eat cake!' You can? Well, then you're probably strong enough to read on and discover how mistaken so many of our most cherished beliefs turn out to be.

Marie Antoinette did not say 'Let them eat cake'. The phrase was attributed to her by those in opposition to Louis XVI and first gained currency thirty years before when Jean Jacques Rousseau had a Princess declare 'Let them eat *brioches*' in a fictitious story of his.

★

Contrary to popular belief, the 'goose-step' is not a German invention. Indeed it was introduced by the British Army. A commanding officer devised the step to enable him to see if any of his men were drunk.

★

An ostrich does not bury its head in the sand when it is frightened or wants to hide. It only does so when it is covering its eggs for protection, or searching for food.

★

Rats don't desert a sinking ship. They are unable to predict disaster, so if a ship happens to sink they will go down with it.

★

Many people remove flowers from a sick room every night in the mistaken belief that they are dangerous. In fact the amount of carbon dioxide given off by flowers at night is so small that even a vast quantity of blooms would make absolutely no difference to the room's oxygen content. Curiously there are trained nurses who still believe in removing flowers at night, even though Florence Nightingale realised the fallacy a century ago.

★

Catgut does not come from cats. It comes from sheep.

★

Do you believe you should 'feed a cold and starve a fever?' You do? Well, you needn't bother. It's a popular belief that has no scientific basis. Whether you have a cold or a fever it seems you are better off eating your normal diet. Eating too much food may make you fat, whereas too little will mean lack of energy.

★

Camel hair brushes are not made from camel's hair, but from squirrel's hair.

★

The legend that Cleopatra committed suicide by clasping an asp to her bosom has been in existence since the very time of her death, even though Plutarch says she actually had a hollow bodkin containing poison which she pushed into her left arm. The rumours began when the Roman general Octavian rode in triumph through the streets of Rome, followed by a chariot containing a figure of the dead Cleopatra on a couch. Entwined around her was a model of an asp.

★

A pineapple is not a pine or an apple: it is a berry. And a potato is neither a vegetable nor a fruit, but a root.

★

Everybody knows about Cinderella and her beautiful glass slippers. But not everybody knows that the original Cinders *never* wore glass slippers. She had *fur* slippers instead. The mistake came about in 1697 when the story was translated from the original French of Charles Perrault. According to Perrault Cinderella wore '*pantoufles en vair*', but the translator mistook '*vair*' for '*verre*', meaning glass, so for the last three hundred years Cinderella has worn glass slippers.

★

Spaghetti did not originate in Italy, but came from China. It was imported to Italy in the thirteenth century by the explorer Marco Polo.

★

'A red rag to a bull' is meaningless – because bulls are colour blind.

★

When lying in the hot sun on the beach the last thing you need to cool you down is an ice-cream – the reason being that ice-cream actually makes you warmer. This is because it contains sugar and carbohydrates which, when taken into the body, are oxidized, giving off heat.

★

Although it may sound contradictory (and even smell contradictory) garlic belongs to the lily family.

★

There is no soda in soda water. It is charged with carbon dioxide like other 'sparkling' drinks.

★

The Emperor Nero did not fiddle while Rome burned. Fiddles had not been invented, and at the time of the fire he was fifty miles away at his villa.

★

Some people believe that all animals sit or lie down to sleep. Not at all. Horses, elephants, zebras and antelopes are among many animals who can sleep standing up.

★

There is no scientifically sound reason for baiting mousetraps with cheese. Mice like food of all sorts and have no special preference for cheese.

★

Chop suey isn't a Chinese dish. It originated in California.

★

Charles Lindbergh was not the first person to fly non-stop across the Atlantic. He was the sixty-seventh, though he was the first to do it alone.

*

Mustard gas is not a gas; neither is it mustard. It is a volatile liquid.

*

Children are often told: 'An apple a day keeps the doctor away.' The phrase originated because apples contain Vitamin C, but there is no real evidence that Vitamin C will actually prevent illness, and even if it does, there are many fruits, such as oranges, which have a much higher percentage of the vitamin within them. What's more, the old idea that eating apples will keep your teeth healthy is now considered a fallacy as well, as it is said that the natural sugar content that apples leave in your mouth results in tooth decay. Some dentists say that peanuts are much better because they cause the saliva glands to secrete more saliva and so keep the mouth clean.

*

The Belgian hare is not a hare. It is a rabbit.

*

There is no rice in rice-paper. It is made from pitch or wood pulp.

*

Wormwood is not a wood; neither is it a worm. It is an aromatic plant.

*

The primrose is not a rose. The name is derived from the French *'prime rolles'* – 'earliest little flowers'.

*

Snakes cannot be charmed by music because they have no ears and are deaf to music. However, they can feel vibration and so it is possible that they respond to a snake-charmer's foot tapping rather than his music.

*

The North Pole is usually considered to be the coldest place on earth, but the coldest temperatures ever recorded have been in Verkhoyansk in Northern Siberia where it has been 90° *below* zero.

*

The centipede doesn't have a hundred legs: it usually has 21 or 30, though some have *more* than 100. And millipedes certainly don't have a thousand legs: very few have more than 200.

*

It is changes of temperature, light and fear that make a chameleon change colour rapidly – not a change in the colour of its surroundings.

*

It's a mistake to say the moon shines. It doesn't. It has no light of its own and so only reflects the light of the sun.

*

At school, children are still taught that King John signed the Magna Carta. Well, King John did *not* sign the Magna Carta because he was unable to write. What he actually did was *seal* it with wax.

*

St Patrick, the patron saint of Ireland, was not Irish at all, but a Frenchman.

Throughout the centuries, many statues and pictures of Queen Boadicea depict her riding on a chariot with scythes on the chariot axles. It is very unlikely that she did so; first, because there is no evidence that such a weapon was in use at that particular time, and second, if it was intended to chop off the legs of the Romans as she rode along, it is more than likely that her own soldiers and horses would have lost limbs too.

*

If you know Shakespeare's play *Richard III*, you will probably think of King Richard as a hump-backed monster with a withered arm. The truth of the matter is that his physique was perfectly normal. Portraits of him, his suit of armour, and contemporary reports of his skill in sports, all indicate that he was in no way deformed. It was the Tudors who put it about that he was a grotesque. Shortly after his death there was even a rumour that he was two years in his mother's womb before she had the nerve to unleash him on the world.

# GOLDWYNISMS

**'For years I have been known for saying 'include me out', but today I am giving it up forever.'** *Samuel Goldwyn*, at Balliol College, Oxford, 1 March 1945.

Samuel Goldwyn (1882-1974) had a winning way with words. Polish by birth, he became an American citizen and one of the legendary Hollywood film moguls. Almost as memorable as the great MGM pictures he produced were the great verbal clangers he created...

An agent once tried to sell Goldwyn a prominent actor. Goldwyn replied that he was not interested in established stars: he wanted to build his own stars instead.

'Look how I developed Jon Hall', said Goldwyn. 'He's a better leading man than Robert Taylor will ever be – some day.'

\*

'A wide screen just makes a bad film twice as bad.'

\*

'Going to call him ''William''? What kind of a name is that? Every Tom, Dick and Harry's called William. Why don't you call him Bill?'

\*

'In two words: im-possible.'

\*

'Every director bites the hand that lays the golden egg.'

\*

'A verbal contract isn't worth the paper it's written on.'

\*

'You ought to take the bull between the teeth.'

\*

'We're overpaying him but he's worth it.'

\*

'Why should people go out and pay good money to see

bad films when they can stay at home and see bad television for nothing?'

★

'We have all passed a lot of water since then.'

★

'How'm I gonna do decent pictures when all my good writers are in jail? ... Don't misunderstand me, they all ought to be hung.'

★

'Chaplin is no businessman – all he knows is he can't take anything less.'

★

'We want a story that starts with an earthquake and works its way up to a climax.'

★

'My Toujours Lautrec!'

★

'Tell me, how did you love my picture?'

★

'Yes, my wife's hands are very beautiful. I'm going to have a bust made of them.'

★

'Anybody who goes to see a psychiatrist ought to have his head examined.'

★

'Why only twelve disciples? Go out and get thousands.'

★

'Gentlemen, I want you to know that I am not always right, but I am never wrong.'

★

'If Roosevelt were alive he'd turn over in his grave.'

★

'I'll give you a definite maybe.'

★

'The reason why so many people turned up at Louis B. Mayer's funeral was they wanted to make sure he was dead.'

★
'It's more than magnificent – it's mediocre.'

★
'If you cannot give me your word of honour will you give me your promise?'

★
*When told that a story was rather caustic he replied:*
'I don't care what it costs. If it's good, we'll make it.'

★
*Of a book:*
'I read part of it all the way through.'

★
*Of a piece of dialogue:*
'Let's have some new clichés.'

★
'A bachelor's life is no life for a single man.'

★

# HITTING THE HEADLINES

**'SIXTY HORSES WEDGED IN CHIMNEY
The story to fit this sensational headline has not turned up
yet.'**

*J.B. Morton* (1893-1973)

There have been real stories to go with all the real
headlines that follow – but the stories didn't quite fit the
headlines because the headlines didn't quite say what
they meant to say. Usually, thanks to an innocent
misprint or a not-so-innocent sub-editor, they said
rather more than they intended...

**Officer Convicted of Accepting Bride**

★

MAN FOUND DEAD IN GRAVEYARD

★

**Troops Watch Orange March**

★

GIRL WITH A DETECTIVE IN HER BOOT

★

*LOCAL MAN HAS LONGEST HORNS IN TEXAS*

★

**Passengers Hit By Cancelled Trains**

★

BUFFALO SWEPT OFF FEET BY
MENDELSSOHN CHOIR

★

EX-ALDERMAN DIES – *ONE OF EIGHT AXED
BY TORIES*

★

**Massive Organ Draws The Crowd**

★

HAMM FAILS TO IDENTIFY YEGGS

★

*BRIDE OF FOUR MOUTHS SUES HUSBAND*

★

DOG IN BED SEEKS DIVORCE

★

SISTERS WED BROTHERS HAVE BABIES SAME DAY

★

**Man Is Fatally Murdered**

★

*BARE FEET AND TINTED TONSILS WITH SANDALS*

★

**Police Move in Book Case**

★

RICHARD BURTON TO TEACH ENGLISH AT OFORXD

★

UNDERTAKER'S FAILURE – *LET DOWN BY CUSTOMERS*

★

*THREE BATTERED IN FISH SHOP MAN GAOLED FOR ASSAULT*

★

**20-Year Friendship Ends at the Altar**

★

ANNUAL FAT CATTLE SHOW 300 ALDER-MEN MARCH TO CHURCH

★

**Newly Weds Aged 82, Have Problem**

★

*WIFE DIED AFTER ATTEMPTING TO COMMIT SUICIDE*

★

*MONTY FLIES BACK TO FRONT*

★

**Lucky Man Sees Friends Die**

★

MAN RECOVERING AFTER FATAL
ACCIDENT

★

STRIP CLUB SHOCK
*MAGISTRATES MAY ACT ON INDECENT
SHOWS*

★

**Sterility May be Inherited**

★

BOY COOKS MUST EAT OWN VITALS

★

HOTEL BURNS DOWN: *TWO HUNDRED
GUESTS ESCAPE HALF GLAD*

★

ENRAGED BULL INJURES FARMER WITH
AXE

★

*BACHELORS PREFER BEAUTY TO BRAINS IN
THEIR WIVES*

★

**Farmer's Eight-hour Vigil in Bog**

★

**Greenland Volcano in Eruption:**
*BY ARRANGEMENT WITH THE TIMES*

★

FALSE CHARGE OF THEFT OF HENS
POLICE ON A WILD GOOSE CHASE

★

TREATED LIKE A DOG BY WIFE
*Husband cooked for thirty years*

★

**Man Denies Committing Suicide**

★

PRISONERS ESCAPE AFTER EXECUTION

★

*MORE MEN FOUND WEDDED THAN WOMEN*

★

## PEER'S SEAT BURNS ALL NIGHT
### *ANCIENT PILE DESTROYED*

★

### Council 'Digging Own Grave'
## SMALLER BODY URGED

★

## 'STRIPPED GIRL'
### Yard to probe

★

### *MOUNTING PROBLEMS FOR NEWLY WEDS*

★

## BOLTING HORSE SAVED AFTER FALL OFF PONY

★

### Onion Prospects Reported Strong

★

### Father of Ten Shot Dead
### *Mistaken for Rabbit*

★

## ARCHDEACON TURNS SOD

★

## BIG PETWORTH WIN FOR QUEEN
### *Major success for Windsor cow*

★

## PORTERS MARCH OVER ASIAN IMMIGRANTS

★

### Nudist Arrested
### *UNCLOTHED MAN, WHO ADMITS BRANDISHING PISTOL, IS CHARGED WITH CARRYING CONCEALED WEAPON*

★

## DEAD POLICEMEN IN THE FORCE FOR 18 YEARS

★

### *WOMEN ARE BECOMING MORE BEAUTIFUL MEN, ALSO LOOKING BETTER*

★

WOMAN KICKED BY HER HUSBAND SAID
TO BE GREATLY IMPROVED

★

EVANS SAYS PUTTING MAN TO DEATH
ELIMINATES HOPE OF REHABILITATION

★

Southport a Town of Old People
*ONE IN SIX OVER 65 GRAVE PROBLEM*

★

Peace or War Deemed Near

★

*'LEONORE' ONLY OPERA BEETHOVEN
WROTE ON MONDAY EVENING*

★

FOUL PLAY SUSPECTED IN DEATH OF MAN
FOUND HANDLESS, BOUND AND HANGED

★

RURAL COUNCIL DISTRICT BIRTHRATE
HIGHEST FOR TEN YEARS – HUMAN KILLER
ADOPTED

★

*VOLUNTARY WORKERS STRIKE FOR
HIGHER PAY*

★

Channel Swim Attempt
*BOSTON GIRL'S ARRIVAL IN LIVERPOOL*

★

POLICE FOUND SAFE UNDER BLANKET

★

Senate Passes Death Penalty
*MEASURE PROVIDES FOR ELECTROCUTION
FOR ALL PERSONS OVER 17*

★

Motorist Heavily Penalised
SUSPENDED FROM THE WHEEL FOR A YEAR

★

Council Claim Street was Demolished by Accident

★

47

## GOING TO AUSTRALIA FOR A WEE HONEY-MOON?

*If we can fit it in says couple*

*

## PROTESTOR TRIED TO SPOIL PLAY BUT THE ACTORS SUCCEEDED

*

## *NINETY YEAR OLD MAN CHARGED WITH RAPE CHANGES PLEA TO 'GUILTY'*

*

### Ex-Beauty Queen Admits She is a Woman

*

## *EDITORS BLAME TYPE-SETTERS FOR INAKURATE SPELING*

*

# IT PAYS TO ADVERTISE

**'One ad is worth more to a paper than forty editorials.'**
*Will Rogers* (1879-1935)

And one small ad gone wrong is worth more to a reader than forty strip cartoons! Whether it's a matter of a subtle misprint or a brazen bloomer, so long as it sounds all wrong to mistaike-lovers it sounds all right...

'Wanted: SINGLE MAN or GIRL for STUD FARM. Girl must be twenty-five or over and experienced.' (*Worthing Gazette and Herald*)

*

'FOR SALE: Direct from the manufacturer, human hair wigs. Cut out the middle man – 100% cheaper.' (*London Evening Standard*)

*

'Silk? Tweed? Hopsack? Worsted? No matter what your topcoat is made of, this miracle spray will make it really repellent.' (*Birmingham Evening Mail*)

*

'Deep freeze meat: best Scotch meat from Wales.' (*Edinburgh Evening News*)

*

'Cordon Bleu cook required for government department dining room. Good salary, excellent working conditions, plus luncheon vouchers.' (*Guardian*)

*

'Surgical instruments: complete assortment of deceased surgeons.' (*British Medical Journal*)

*

'Two business ladies require sleeping partner for beauty salon.' (*Liverpool Echo*)

*

'Lady required for 6 hours work per week to clean small
officers at Station Road, Witney.'
(*Witney & West Oxfordshire Gazette*)

'Piano: Would suit beginner with chipped legs.'
(*Western Morning News*)

*

'FOR SALE: Three bra electric fire. Perfect condition.
No plug. £5.' (*Manx Life*)

*

'Austrian/German/Swiss chefs required for new
French restaurant.' (*Evening News*)

*

'Widows made to order. Send us your specifications.'
(*Ely Standard*)

*

'STRADIVARIUS violin for sale cheap. Almost
new.' (*Music and Musicians*)

*

'A young woman wants washing or cleaning three days
a week.' (*Lancashire Evening Telegraph*)

*

'SEXI-DETACHED HOUSES. Almost new.
£15,000.' (*Dalton's Weekly*)

*

'To let: fully furnished self-contained flatlet: £80 per
calendar month: centrally heated, electricity, rats
included.' (*Coventry Evening Telegraph*)

*

'20 MILES from London, lovely little gentleman's
week-end cottage.' (*Country Life*)

*

'Girl wanted for petrol pump attendant.'
(*Cambridge Evening News*)

*

'WANTED – Modern gas cooker suitable for bachelor
with white enamelled sides.' (*Gay News*)

*

'Small flatlet available mid-August, suitable for two
business ladies, use of communal kitchen or two
gentlemen.' (*Cumberland Herald*)

★

'FOR SALE: Doctor's sailing dinghy and accessories. Doctor no further use.' (*Yorkshire Post*)

★

'Afghan Hound for sale – What am I offered for this one-year-old dog? House-trained, gentle, will eat anything and is especially fond of children.'
(*Essex Chronicle*)

★

'WANTED: A mahogany living-room table by a lady.'
(*Homes & Gardens*)

★

'SHEER stockings – designed for evening wear, but so serviceable that lots of women wear nothing else.'
(*Daily Mirror*)

★

'Experienced Au Pair Girl, experienced in housework. Especially enjoys cooing.' (*Evening Standard*)

★

'UNEMPLOYED man seeks work. Completely honest and trustworthy, will take anything.' (*Farmer's Weekly*)

★

'TO LET – furnished room for lady. Semi-private bath. Phone evenings only.' (*Hartsville Messenger*)

★

'WANTED: A first class male waitress. Only qualified persons considered.' (*Montreal Star*)

★

'WANTED URGENTLY: Male or Female serving person for top London nightclub. Must fit uniform 40" bust.' (*New Evening Standard*)

★

'Unusual opportunity for car salesman with initiative and drive. Must have had at least two years experience within last six months or do not apply.' (*Manchester Evening News*)

★

'LOST an antique brooch depicting Venus in Shepherds Bush on Saturday Night.' (*Kensington Post*)

★

'WANTED – A reliable young woman to cook, wash, iron and milk two cows.' (*Auckland News*)

★

'Amazing offer. Fish and chip fryer, made from chip-resistant enamel.' (*Dalton's Weekly*)

★

'ENGAGEMENTS: Bernard and Sybil would like to announce their engagement due to unforeseen circumstances. Other commiserations.' (*Tampa Morning Tribune*)

*

'WANTED – to trade violin for shotgun.'
(*Portsmouth Evening News*)

*

'ACCOMODATION includes large split-level lounge, with large bay window overlooking seperate WC.' (*Matlock Mercury*)

*

'GOD is your refuge, your very strength in times of trouble. Please write Box 4131.' (*Christian Record*)

*

'Please note. Rings can be ordered by post. Simply state size required or enclose string tied around your finger.' (*Townswoman*)

*

'TO SELL – 4-door Sedan complete with actress. Call 5-8342.' (*Philadelphia Enquirer*)

*

'Small bungalow for sale, kitchen/dining room, bath & WC, bedroom and loving room.' (*Perth Daily News*)

*

'SECRETARY required. Shorthand essential, but not absolutely necessary.' (*Yorkshire Post*)

*

'FOR SALE – Delicate porcelain statuette. Victorian, belongs to elderly lady slightly cracked.'
(*Essex Weekly News*)

*

'Have your portrait painted at your own convenience.'
(*Dundee Evening Telegraph and Post*)

*

'FOR SALE: Beautiful Wedding dress – Size 18 – only worn twice.' (*Kansas City News*)

*

'Young lady required in accounts office, previous experience not essential; bust be able to type.'
(*Kensington Post*)

*

'Delightful country cottage, 2 bedrooms, large lounge, diner kitchen, bathroom, coloured suite, toilet 5 miles Chichester.' (*Worthing Herald*)

★

'BACHELOR (45), non-driver, would accompany same on car tour of Scottish highlands.' (*Lancashire Evening Telegraph*)

★

'Excellent vintage wines for sale, property of a lady removed from a cellar after many years.' (*Petersfield Post*)

★

'Hammers for sale – bulk purchase, would suit any handyman with claw head.' (*Dublin Evening Herald*)

★

'Fifteen-foot travel trailer. Boat rack built on top, complete with wench.' (*Practical Boat Owner*)

★

'Bicycle available for quick sale, looked after by young lady owner with collapsible frame.' (*New Zealand Outdoor*)

★

'Honeymoons, from now on £50 per person; quiet and central, hot and cold, separate tables, children catered for.' (*South Wales Echo*)

★

'Lost: a pink see-through nightdress. Somewhere on the M1.' (*Herts and Essex Observer*)

★

'Lady with deaf aid wishes to meet man with contact lenses.' (*Kern Valley Sun*)

★

'WANTED to trade one saxophone for cow in fancy case.' (*Pueblo Chieftain*)

★

'FOR SALE: Sheraton table, property of titled lady, with exquisitely carved legs.' (*New Homemaker*)

★

'FOR SALE: To a good owner, fully grown and domesticated leopard. Able to roam free and untied, will eat flesh from the hand. Offers please.'
(*Calcutta paper*)

★

'Home urgently needed for cow. Marriage broken cannot afford to keep her.' (*Dairy Farmer*)

★

# JENUINE MISTAKES

**'He respects Owl, because you can't help respecting anybody who can spell Tuesday, even if he doesn't spell it right.'**
*A.A. Milne, The House at Pooh Corner*

Even the best-educated individuals make spelling mistakes. The trouble starts at school when, at a very early age, we're told that 'reading, writing, and arithmetic' all begin with an 'R'. From then on things can only go from badd to werse.

Recently my small son arrived home from school feeling very pleased with himself: he had just become top of the class. His teacher had asked if anyone could pronounce the word spelt C-h-i-h-u-a-h-u-a, and nobody could, until suddenly my boy sneezed. 'Well done!' said the teacher.

Even when children can spell a word they don't always know what it means. A fourth-former I know was asked to spell matrimony.

'M-a-t-r-i-m-o-n-y' said the girl immediately.

'Now define it', replied the teacher.

'Well, I'm not sure what it is, but I do know that my mother's had enough of it.'

Of course, it's not only school children who can't spell. Recently I was looking at an appallingly typed letter that a colleague had given me to read.

'Your secretary spells atrociously', I said.

'Does she?' was his answer. 'Well, if she does it's the only word she *can* spell.'

To give you a flavour/flavor of how bad some people's spelling can be, here are two dozen howlers garnered from schools in Britain and America:

'The Indians live very froogley.'

'I allso wish you a happy new deckade.'

★

'My friend and I visited the Dolldrums.'

★

'I hate school dinners, speshally Tabby oaker.'

★

'We took the temprature in farren height.'

★

'My sister moved to Pencil vanea.'

★

'The cistern chapel is where Mickel Angelo painted the selling.'

★

'We really don't care enuff about nateral fenominum.'

★

'He through the ball up on to the parrowpet.'

★

'We could not use it any more as it was all mestup.'

★

'It dunt marrer anymore.'

★

'Although our societies are formed by man, he isn't able to flunksuate with its pace.'

★

'Surprisingly enough this is the first parragraff I have written about conjewgal writes.'

★

'My next store naybore has gone to hospital for a historecktome.'

★

'I don't like being taken for granite.'

★

'Your Dad sayed you didnt ort to keep goin off to these forren parts and leavin Sinthear behind.'

★

'The West-women's doubles team brought the team back from a four-game deficate.'

*

'I am told that the haunted tower does not actually exist, it is purely a mith.'

*

'I am feeling very angches about the outcome of the court case.'

*

'I have been suffering recently from dan druff and a tempra mentall pidjon. Eversince dan moved next door there has been no piece.'

*

'The stewdress served cocktails on the plain.'

*

'Whoreship in the modern church.'

*

'Plastick surjons make you pay through the nose.'

*

'That's the way it supostube.'

Some say that today's children are such poor spellers because of the less disciplined approach of today's teachers. Well, here is the work of a child from 'the good old days', the bygone era when 'standards' were much more strictly maintained ...

### BOYS by Lucy

Boys bother yer, they don't let you have no peace. Girls can't sit quiet in a room and talk secrets if boys is about. They come behind yer and lissen, and then they bust out laffin, and make yer jump. They're awful rood are boys.

Boys ave no maternal instinct that girls ave. They don't understand girls likin dolls. It's fare shameful the way which a boy pulls a doll about by the legs and arms, they stick pins into the poor things and fist them to make them squaek.

If a boy has is frends in, they turn the ouse upside

down. Boys is unkind, they av'nt no feelins, they're diffrent to girls. They don't cry when they're urt if girls is about.

Boys are awful sorry when they urt girls, but they soon forget it, they are so ard arted. Boys koff and em at girls in the street. When girls laff, boys make redikalus noises, and carry on right rood.

Boys are not always gettin in and out of frends like girls. When boys get out of frends they stops out. Boys make fun of girls and trys to snub them and put them down, but they can't. Muther says women are sperior intellecks to men, and that's why.

Some boys are reel nice and walk ome with yer from school, and carry yer things, but then they keep lettin them fall and vesc yer, and they don't stick to yer long.

Boys don't want to stop in the house when there's cookin to be done and elp, but it dozzen do, they are too greedy. Boys can't rustrain their appytites like what girls can.

I like boys.


If you want to see how your spelling compares with that of the average school-leaver today, get someone to read you the list of words that follows and discover how many of the words you can spell faultlessly. The list is based on a survey organised by a group of British teachers and designed to find the most commonly misspelt words in the English language. Or is it misspelled?

A  access  accessible  accommodation
   achievement  advantageous  aerial  amount
   arguing  auxiliary

B  beautiful  believe  benefited  business

C  ceiling  changeable  commit  committed
   comparison  conceit  condemn  conscientious
   conscious  corroborate  coolly  courageous

60

**D** deceive definitely disappear disappoint describe description desirable development dissatisfied dissatisfying drunkenness

**E** Edinburgh eligible embarrass encyclopaedia excessive exaggerate exhilaration existence

**F** February forty

**G** gauge grammar gramophone grievous guard

**H** handkerchiefs heifer humour humorous

**I** immediate incidentally independent indispensable irrelevant

**J** judge judgment

**K** knowledge knowledgeable

**L** leisure likeable lovable

**M** managerial marriage Mediterranean Middlesbrough mischief mischievous miscellaneous

**N** necessary necessarily neighbour newsstand niece ninety noticeable

**O** occur occurrence organiser

**P** panic panicked parallel pastime perseverance persistent predecessor possessive prescription privilege proceeding (preceding) professor pronounce pronunciation pursue pursuer

**Q** queue queueing

**R** receive receipt recommend rhyme rhythm ridiculous

**S** secretary secretarial seize separate sergeant siege similar sincere succeed success

**T**  theatre  thorough  till (until)  tranquillity
transfer  transference  transferred  tyranny
tyrant  true  truly

**U**  umbrella

**V**  vegetable  vicious  view

**W**  Wednesday  weird  whole  wholly

**Y**  yacht  yield

# KINQUERING KONGS

**'It was no spooner read than soaken.'**

The Reverend William Archibald Spooner (1844-1930) was Warden of New College, Oxford from 1903 to 1927. In 1879, on a day that changed the whole history of the English language, Dr Spooner rose to his feet during a service in the College chapel and announced the next hymn as '*Kinquering Kongs their titles take*'. And so the 'Spoonerism' was born. Since then countless more 'spoonerisms' have been attributed to the great man. Whether he actually said any of them or not, nobody knows (and very few care), but they are sun all the fame. Here are the best ...

'Let us toast the queer old Dean.'

*

'You have been caught fighting a liar in the quad.'

*

'Sir, you have tasted two whole worms.'

*

'You have hissed all my mystery lectures.'

*

'You will leave Oxford on the next town drain.'

*

'I do apologise, I am afraid I was sewn into this sheet.'

*

'I remember your name perfectly, but I just can't think of your face.'

*

'But I am not so think as you drunk I am.'

*

'Excuse me, you are occupewing my pie.'

*

'Give me a well-boiled icycle.'

★

'It's roaring with pain outside.'

★

'I have just received a blushing crow.'

★

'Is the bean dizzy?'

★

'I tried to stroke it, but it popped on its draws and ran out of the room.'

★

'I have in my breast a half-warmed fish.'

★

The accidental transposition of words did not end with Dr Spooner's death in 1930. In March 1981, Simon Groom, presenter of the popular BBC children's television programme *Blue Peter*, informed the viewers that next week they would be looking at: '... blind dogs for the guide.'

# LITERARY LAPSES

**'The errors of great men are venerable because they are more fruitful than the truths of little men.'**
*Nietzsche (1844-1900)*

You don't need to be able to read between the lines to discover that some of the greatest masters of world literature were guilty of the most deplorable literary lapses. What on earth were they thinking about when they allowed themselves to write what follows...

'A man who exposes himself when he is intoxicated, has not the art of getting drunk.'
*from* Life of Samuel Johnson *by James Boswell*

★

'As big as any man could wish to have, and lined inside, and double-lined in the lower parts, and an extra piece of stiffening at the bottom.'
*from* Under the Greenwood Tree *by Thomas Hardy*

★

'You think me a queer fellow already. It's not easy either, to tell you what I feel, not easy for so queer a fellow as I to tell you in how many ways he's queer.'
*from* A Passionate Pilgrim *by Henry James*

★

'Well,' said the Duchess to me, 'apart from your balls can't I be of any use to you?'
*from* Cities of the Plain *by Marcel Proust*

★

'She gave a little scream and a jerk, and so relieved herself...'
*from* The Duke's Children *by Anthony Trollope*

★

'... In Winter his private balls were numerous enough for any young lady who was not suffering under the insatiable appetite for fifteen.'
*from* Sense and Sensibility *by Jane Austen*

'Oh, I can't explain!' cried Roderick impatiently, returning to his work. 'I've only one way of expressing my deepest feelings – it's this.' And he swung his tool.

*from* Roderick Hudson *by Henry James*

★

'Prince of the school, he had gained an easy dominion over the old Greek master by the fascination of his parts.'

*from* Marius the Epicurean *by Walter Pater*

★

'On entering the drawing-room, she found the whole party at loo, and was immediately invited to join them...'

*from* Pride and Prejudice *by Jane Austen*

★

It has been suggested that there was far more to the relationship between Sherlock Holmes and Dr Watson than meets the eye, a rumour that began because Doyle made the mistake of writing:

'During my life I (Dr Watson) related over sixty cases from which it is apparent how gifted my friend Sherlock Holmes was. But together we also experienced things which have not been made public for reasons of discretion. These adventures were of a delicate nature and could give offence...'

★

'Some great men owe most of their greatness to the ability of detecting in those they destine for their tools the exact quality of strength that matters for their work...'

*from* Lord Jim *by Joseph Conrad*

★

'Now the time was coming when I began to think about helping princesses by fetching their balls up from the bottom.'

*from* Praeterita *by John Ruskin*

★

'Mr Grant, really quite glad of an excuse to dismount, offered his cock to Lydia, who immediately flung a leg over it, explaining that she had put on a frock with pleats on purpose.'
*from* The Brandons *by Angela Thirkell*

★

'The organ 'gins to swell;
She's coming, she's coming!
My lady comes at last.'
*from* At the Church Gate *by William Makepeace Thackeray*

★

'She realised at last that she had no vocation for struggling with her combinations.'
*from* The Portrait of a Lady *by Henry James*

'That confidence which presumes to do, by surveying the surface, what labour only can perform, by penetrating the bottom.'
*from* Preface to Shakespeare *by Samuel Johnson*

*

'All my heart
Went forth to embrace him coming
ere he came.'
*from* Oenone *by Alfred Lord Tennyson*

*

'Mrs Ray declared that she had not found it all hard and then – with a laudable curiosity, seeing how little she had known about balls, desired to have an immediate account of Rachel's doings.'
*from* Rachel Ray *by Anthony Trollope*

*

'He had a spectacle case in his hand, which he turned over and over while he was thus in question, with a certain free use of thumb which is never seen but in a hand accustomed to tools.'
*from* Little Dorrit *by Charles Dickens*

*

'PS I like my balls very well, and have also received the money.'
*from a letter by William Hazlitt to his mother*

*

'She touched his organ, and from that bright epoch, even it, the old companion of his happiest hours, incapable as he had thought of elevation, began a new and deified existence.'
*from* Martin Chuzzlewit *by Charles Dickens*

*

'He flourished his tool. The end of the lash just touched my forehead. A warm excited thrill ran through my veins, my blood seemed to give a bound, and then raced fast and hot along its channels. I got up nimbly, came round to where he stood, and faced him.'
*from* The Professor *by Charlotte Brontë*

'Mrs Glegg had doubtless the glossiest and crispest brown curls in her drawers, as well as curls in various degrees of fuzzy laxness.'
*from* The Mill on the Floss *by George Eliot*

★

'It's just like Longueville, you know.' Gordon Wright went on: 'He always comes at you from behind; he's so awfully fond of surprises.'
*from* Confidence *by Henry James*

★

# MAGNIFICENT MISPRINTS

**'Love truth, but pardon error.'**
*Voltaire* (1694-1778)

The world's press is noted for its wonderful ability to misquote, misprint, and misunderstand absolutely everything. If you've ever had anything to do with an event that's been written up in the paper, I guarantee (well, almost) that there was at least one error in the report. There's no point in sulking about it: you've just got to face life as it is and make the most of it. After all, the misprints usually add a little extra something to a story ...

'**Today's weather:** A depression will mope across Southern England.' (*The Guardian*)

\*

'The landlord insisted that no female should be allowed in the bra without a man.' (*Glasgow Herald*)

\*

'Miss Patricia Muddleton, qualified vice instructor, sang, *Christian, Dost Thou See Them?* on Sunday night.' (*Yorkshire Post*)

\*

'The jury were informed that during the evening Maloney spat in Flannigan's face and called him a 'stinking Ulsterman'. Flannigan punched Maloney, and O'Reilly hit him over the head with a chair. Maloney kicked O'Reilly in the groin and threw his drink over Flannigan. This led to slight ill-feeling and they began to fight, the defending counsel claimed today.' (*Belfast Newsletter*)

\*

'Mrs Alsop was married before anaesthetics came into use in surgical operations.'
(*Cumberland Evening News*)

'It was announced today that the wedding would take place on July 3rd at St Mary's Church. Betting 9-4 against, 6-1, 10-1.' (*Manchester Evening News*)

\*

'I never went through that ghastly adolescent phase most girls experience. I went from child to woman in one go. One day I was a child. The next, a man.' (*Woman and Home*)

\*

'Mrs Freda Wallace Brown, 79, of Burlington Avenue, dined this week at her home. Service and cremation will be held next Thursday at 2.00pm. (*Accrington Weekly*)

\*

'For cockroaches do not use sodium fluoride, as children or cherished pets may eat the sodium fluoride instead of the cockroaches.' (*Ludlow Tribune*)

\*

'Never throw away old chicken bones, or those left from a roast. Put them in water and boil them for several hours with a few diced vegetables, it will make very delicious soap.' (*New Zealand Woman's Weekly*)

\*

'Two men were admitted to hospital suffering from mild buns.' (*Essex Chronicle*)

\*

'The bride was gowned in white silk and lace. The colour scheme of the bridesmaids' gowns and flowers was punk.' (*Toronto Post*)

\*

'A set of traffic lights has been stolen from a main road junction in Exeter. A police spokesman said: "Some thieves will stop at nothing." ' (*Exeter Express & Echo*)

\*

'The accident occurred at Hillcrest Drive and Santa Barbara Avenue as the dead man was crossing the intersection.' (*Los Angeles Times*)

★

'The ladies of St Martins Church have discarded clothing of all kinds. Call at 152 North Street for inspection. Mrs Freeman will be willing to oblige you in any way she can.' (*Worthing Gazette*)

★

'The murder of the man and the finding of the body was followed by a series of tragedies, including the suicide of the murdered man.' (*Boston Post*)

★

'The Women's Institute will hold their fortnightly lecture in St Mary's Hall, the topic will be "Country Life" when Mrs Wills will show slides of some beautiful wild pants.' (*Matlock Mercury*)

★

'In a bitterly cold wind, the Queen, wearing a warm sage-green tweed coat with a beaver lamb collar and a green mitre-installation of turbo-alternators and boilers.' (*Thames Water News*)

★

'An Arab country, like Ireland, is a place where the remarkable seldom happens, and the impossible is of frequent occurrence.' (*New Zealand Times*)

★

'Many students are planning to follow the team to the scene of the bottle.' (*International Herald Tribune*)

★

'Mr Bromsgrove suffered a stroke on 24 November 1980 but with the loving care of his family and his kind and efficient nurse, he never fully recovered.'
(*Crewe Chronicle*)

★

'Ernest Hemingway who made Pamplona's annual fiesta famous, is to have a street there named after him.'
(*The Daily Telegraph*)

★

'The speaker told of her perilous experience with a bra constrictor.' (*Methodist Recorder*)

'The ladies of the Helping Hand Society enjoyed a swap social on Friday evening. Everybody brought along something they no longer needed. Many of the ladies were accompanied by their husbands.'
(*Arizona Star*)

★

'Miss Sandison, who is only 19, has grown since last year. In patches her form is most impressive.'
(*Edinburgh Evening News*)

★

'ERRORS. No responsibility can be accepted for losses arising from typographical errors. Advertisers are expected to check their smalls to ensure correct appearance.' (*Rhodesia Herald*)

★

' "Fortunately, we are insured against Acts of God", said the Vicar of St Peter's, after lightning struck, sending rafters crashing down on the church altar.'
(*Acton Gazette*)

★

'Unless the teachers receive a higher salary increase they may decide to leave their pests.'
(*Times Educational Supplement*)

★

'Mrs Hudson, whose husband works for British Rail, has two other children, Simon 3½ and Emma 12, but they are not twins.' (*Mother and Baby*)

★

'The service was held at 11.00am by the Rev. John Hamill, whose theme was "Evil Member In The Church". The choir sang the anthem *Who Can It Be*?'
(*Columbus Dispatch*)

★

'Over 50 children took advantage of the mobile clinic and were examined for tuberculosis and other diseases which the clinic offered free of charge.' (*Boston News*)

73

★

'Experts know that the alcoholic process takes longer in men, but the end reshult is just the same.'
(*Holylake News and Advertiser*)

★

'The service ended with the singing of the good old hymn, *All Police That On Earth Do Dwell*.'
(*Toronto Post*)

★

'The Tenth Brigade will be withdrawn next month and will be held in reserve or demoralised.'
(*The West Briton*)

★

'Colonel Marooney, the bottle scarred veteran, died at his home last week aged 82.' (*Wilts Paper*)

★

'It must have been the most melodramatic farewell to be filmed since Bogart said goodbye to Bergman in *Casablanca* as Scotland's World Cup squad at Hampden last night waved farewell to over 35,000 hell wishers.' (*Edinburgh Evening News*)

★

'The council is cutting down on unnecessary postage expenditure by asking householders to collect their rates bill. They will be writing to every householder to inform them of this fact.' (*Bristol Evening News*)

★

'The new bride is approximately eighteen feet wide from buttress to buttress.' (*Baltimore Sun*)

★

'We note with regret that Mr Willis Overing is recovering after a serious car crash.'
(*Toronto Daily Star*)

★

'The new hospital extension will enable patients to be prepared and served in such a way that has previously been impossible.' (*Idaho Post*)

★

'At Panama the sun rises in the Pacific and sets in the Atlantic – due to a gigantic bend in the isthmus.' (*Geographical Journal*)

*

'Recently Mrs Richards invested in a cow, and she is now supplying the whole neighbourhood with milk, butter and eggs.' (*West Sussex Times*)

*

'On making enquiries at the Hospital this afternoon, we learn that the deceased is as well as can be expected.' (*Jersey Evening Post*)

*

'Some of the boy's methods are quite ingenious, the professors at the Institute have found. For instance, when asked to multiply 20 by 24 mentally, he gave the answer – 600 – in a few seconds.' (*Baltimore Sun*)

*

'A pair of socks were ordered to be destroyed by magistrates this week so they cannot again be used for criminal activity.' (*Birmingham Evening Mail*)

*

'It is small wonder that morale is low. Dentists inadequately paid for their work, are pulling out in droves.' (*The Practitioner*)

*

'Sex and violence came into Jane Morgan's life gradually. Then she became a Christian and matters escalated.' (*Essex County Standard*)

*

'Miss Turner has set up a campaign against incestuous relationships at the house in Hydefield Road where she loves with her parents.' (*Enfield Gazette*)

*

'Miss Hampshire is friendly, likeable, and easy to talk to. She has a fine, fair skin which, she admits ruefully, comes out in a mass of freckles at the first hint of sin.' (*Chichester Evening News*)

AT THE END OF
A PERFECT DAY

'Before Miss Pollard concluded the concert with her rendition of *At the end of a perfect day* she was prevented with a large bouquet of carnations from the mayoress.' (*Staffordshire Evening Standard*)

*

'The city which claims to have the largest outdoor mule market in the world recently held a parade of asses led by the governor.' (*New York Magazine*)

*

'Mr Denish Harris, playing solo trumpet in the Bedford Band, was awarded the medal for the best trombone player in the section.' (*Sheffield Telegraph*)

*

'The Prime Minister announced today that the campaign had been a hug success.' (*The Times*)

*

'A police spokesman said that they still had piles to deal with.' (*Leicester Mercury*)

*

'Hero Raaj Kumar has been asking for it and he is getting it in the neck. At last, the chickens have come home to roast for him.' (*Bangladesh Times*)

*

'Police were informed that the robbers menaced Mr Bruce at his garage, one with a wench and the other wielded a revolver.' (*Essex County Standard*)

*

'In a county which has a population of approximately 60,000 there are still only thirty full-time paid employees, of whom twenty-four are assigned to day duty, leaving only six on the night shift.' (*Derbyshire Times*)

*

'Blend sugar, flour, and salt. Add egg and milk, cook until creamy in double boiler. Stir frequently. Add rest of ingredients. Mix well and serve chilled. Funeral services will be held Thursday afternoon at two o'clock.' (*Reedsburg Post*)

*

'An off-licence was looted and police opened fire after they were stoned.' (*Cape Times*)

★

'Before the girls left the White House, Mrs Reagan presented each of them with a small engraving of the Execution Mansion to keep as a memento.'
(*Washington Post*)

★

'We apologise for the error in last week's paper in which we stated that Mr Arnold Dogbody was a defective in the police force. This was a typographical error. We meant, of course, that Mr Dogbody is a detective in the police farce, and are sorry for any embarrassment caused.' (*Ely Standard*)

★

# NOT QUITE NICE

**'Nothing in life is rolled up quicker than the red carpet.'**

You'll find if you go to dinner with the Queen and unfortunately spill your soup, Her Majesty will immediately spill hers too in a courteous attempt to draw attention away from you and your embarrassment.

No mistake is more humiliating than the social gaffe and, unfortunately for us, we don't usually have the Queen on hand to spare our blushes and save the day...

In 1963 the Duke of Edinburgh attended the Kenyan independence celebrations unaccompanied by the Queen. He stood on the podium with the President, Jomo Kenyatta, for the final, ceremonial lowering of the Union Jack.

Just as the flag was about to be lowered, the Prince leaned towards the President and said: 'Are you quite certain you wish to go through with this?' The microphones were still switched on and the vast crowd could not fail to hear what he said.

*

At the turn of the century, Joseph Chamberlain was the guest of honour at a dinner in New York. The Mayor presided, and when coffee was being served the Mayor leaned over to Chamberlain, saying: 'Shall we let the people enjoy themselves a little longer, or had we better have your speech now?'

*

In 1925, when Calvin Coolidge had been elected President of the United States he invited a few friends to dine with him at the White House. The guests felt uneasy in such grand surroundings and in order to ensure that they did everything correctly they decided to emulate every move that Coolidge made.

After the meal the President poured half of his coffee into his saucer – so his guests did likewise. He then poured cream into the coffee and added sugar. The guests did the same. The President then knelt down and laid his saucer on the floor for his cat.

*

After conducting the Halle orchestra one evening in Manchester in 1939, Sir Thomas Beecham returned to his hotel tired and a little irritable. When he entered the foyer he noticed a lady seated on the side nearest the lift and stairs. Sir Thomas recognised her immediately, but was unable to put a name to the face. Knowing that he could not avoid being seen if he tried to go up to his room, he approached her and said:

'Good evening, madam, I do hope you enjoyed the concert?'

He succeeded in carrying on the small talk for a few minutes, without revealing his ignorance of who she was. Just as he was about to take his leave he remembered that she had a brother and asked:

'And tell me, how is your dear brother?'

'He is very well, thank you, Sir Thomas', replied the lady.

'And what's he up to at the moment?'

'Oh, he's still king, you know.'

*

During a visit by Queen Victoria and Prince Albert to Balmoral, the Prince Consort, dressed in a very simple manner, was crossing one of the Scottish lochs in a steamer. He was curious to note everything relating to the management of the vessel, and among other things the cooking. Approaching the galley where a brawny Highlander was attending to culinary matters, he was attracted by the savoury odours of a compound known to Scotsmen as 'Hodge-Podge'.

'What is that?' asked the Prince.

'Hodge-Podge, sir', was the reply.

80

'How is it made?' was the next question.

'Why, there's mutton intil't, and turnips intil't, and carrots intil't, and ...'

'Yes, yes', said the Prince, not realising that 'intil't' meant 'into it'. 'But what is "intil't"? '

'Why, there's mutton intil't, and turnips intil't, and carrots intil't, and...'

'Yes, I see, but what is "intil't"?'

The man looked at him, and seeing that the Prince was serious he replied:

'There's mutton intil't, and turnips intil't, and ...'

'Yes, certainly, I know', urged the inquirer; 'but what is "intil't – intil't"?'

'Why', yelled the Highlander, brandishing his big spoon, 'Am I na tellin' ye what's intil't? There's mutton intil't, and –'

At this point someone else stepped over and explained the situation and the Highlander stood with his mouth wide open in disbelief that he should be wiser than the Prince Consort.

★

A couple of years ago, a crowd of people were sitting in a doctor's waiting room in Birmingham. They had all been waiting a long time when in walked a Pakistani. He was about to go straight into the surgery when a woman jumped up and grabbed his arm, saying in very slow and deliberate English:

'All these people are before you. You take your turn like everyone else. You understand?'

In equally slow and deliberate English the Pakistani said:

'No, you after me. Me doctor. Understand?'

★

The talkative wife of an English diplomat once found herself seated next to a Chinese gentleman at an ambassadorial dinner. Assuming that his lack of conversation was caused by a limited knowledge of English and not her own incessant monologue, the lady

81

spoke to him in a form of pidgin English, which, judging from his smiles and nods, he appeared to comprehend.

She was still talking vivaciously, when the toastmaster 'prayed silence' for his Excellency the Chinese Ambassador – whereupon the man to whom she had been talking rose to his feet and delivered his speech in perfect English. As the applause was dying down afterwards, he whispered in the lady's ear: 'Likee speechee?'

⋆

A former Archbishop of Canterbury paid a visit to New York, and was met by an enthusiastic group of pressmen anxious to know if the Archbishop would be visiting any of New York's famous night clubs on his visit. In an effort at wit and in the hope of avoiding a direct answer, the Archbishop said: 'Are there any night clubs in New York?'

The next day the headlines of all the major newspapers read: 'Archbishop's first question on arrival: ARE THERE ANY NIGHT CLUBS IN NEW YORK?'

⋆

Anxious to meet a distinguished author at a cocktail party, the host's daughter approached the celebrated guest saying: 'Dear Mr Lowell, I understand that your autobiography is going to be published shortly.' 'Posthumously, my dear young lady, posthumously', was the reply.

Uncertain what 'posthumously' meant, she answered; 'Oh, how exciting! I do hope it will be soon.'

⋆

A British diplomat had been invited to a luncheon party at the American Embassy, and during an animated discussion with the host he waved his arms around frantically to emphasise his point. Unfortunately his arm brushed against the head of the host's wife, sending her hair flying across the room and revealing that she was completely bald.

*

A kindly, but very absent-minded, old gentleman was entertaining a party of guests whom he had not seen for some considerable time. Before dinner he approached a young gentleman and asked him how his old friend, the young man's father, was.

'I'm sorry to tell you, sir', replied the young gentleman, 'that my father died six months ago.' The old man expressed his very deep regret and sympathy, and, as the butler announced dinner at that point, they moved into the dining-room.

After the meal the company retired to the drawing-room for coffee and liqueurs. The old man handed the young gentleman a glass of brandy, and enquired after his dear old friend, the young man's father. 'I'm very sorry, sir', replied the man,' but my father is still dead.'

*

When Harold Wilson was in office as Prime Minister there was one memorable moment at a reception at 10 Downing Street. Mrs Mary Wilson was busy entertaining the guests while her husband completed some unfinished work upstairs. The conversation turned to theology and one of the guests remarked: 'Fortunately there is one above who knows all the answers.'

'Oh yes', replied Mrs Wilson, not understanding the significance of the statement, 'Harold will be down in a minute.'

*

# OFFICE ERRORS

**'If all efficiency experts were laid end to end – I'd be in favour of it.'**

*Al Diamond*

However apparently efficient the organisation, however ostensibly high-powered the executives, when two or three are gathered together within easy reach of typewriters, photocopiers, and paperclips, mayhem of sorts is inevitable. Here – found filed under 'm' for 'error' – are some of the myriad of misguided memos, illiterate letters and ambiguous notices to be found in offices all over the land...

---

To/ Thx Idxal Typxwritxr Company.

3rd Dxcxmbxr 198X

Gxntlxmxn,

Wx hxrxby wish to acknowlxdgx thx rxcxipt of your shipmxnt of onx of your xxtra-spxcially quixt typxwritxrs.

Howxvxr, upon opxning thx shipmxnt wx found that for thx timx bxing wx shall bx sxvxrxly handicappxd. In gxnxral, thx typxwritxr is in pxrfxct condition xxcxpt for onx small dxtail. Through somx xrror of assxmbly thxrx sxxms to bx rathxr an xmbarrassing omission – thxrx is no lxttxr on thx machinx for 'x', thx fifth lxttxr of thx alphabxt.

Will you plxasx bx so kind xithxr to sxnd us anothxr machinx or havx this onx sxrvicxd as soon as possiblx.

Sincxrxly,
Xric Xllis, Prxsidxnt,
Thx Xxcxlsior Xxprxss Co.

---

'IN CASE OF FIRE:
ALL STAFF MUST LEAVE THE BUILDING BY
THE APPOINTED FIRE EXITS IN AN
ORDERLY MANNER (UNLESS INDI-
VIDUALLY INSTRUCTED OTHERWISE).'

★

'Members of staff (embracing ladies) are requested not
to loiter in the corridors.'

★

OWING TO THE FUEL CRISIS
OFFICIALS ARE ADVISED TO
TAKE ADVANTAGE OF THEIR
SECRETARIES
BETWEEN THE HOURS OF 12 AND 2.

★

'Staff should empty tea-pots and stand upside down on
tea tray.'

*

'Will gentlemen taking pots of tea on to the lawns please exercise more care. Their hot bottoms are killing the grass.'

*

'If the amount of cash in your paypacket does not agree with the nett wages on your payslip, inform the wages clerk in the Treasurer's Office **before** breaking the seal. No errors can be rectified once the seal is broken.'

*

*Notice seen displayed in bold letters on Xerox machine:*
'THE TYPISTS REPRODUCTION EQUIPMENT IS NOT TO BE INTERFERED WITH WITHOUT PRIOR PERMISSION.'

*

'... It is regretted that we were unable to send the enclosed forms to you before the date by which, had you received them, you would be required to forward completed copies to this office.'

*

Rules for programming the computer:
a) If a programme is useful, change it.
b) Any given programme is obsolete.
c) If a programme seems useless, document it.
d) The value of a programme is proportional to the weight of its output.
e) Programme complexity grows until it exceeds the capability of the programmer.

*

'It has been noted by the management that far too much time is wasted by employees engaged in the practice of visiting the toilet during office hours. In future the following procedure will be adopted:

All personnel will go in alphabetical order, i.e. those with the surnames beginning with the letter 'A' will go from 9.30-9.45; 'B' from 9.45-10.00 and so on.
*Note:* Those of you who are unable to attend at your

appropriate time of day will have to wait until the following day when your turn comes round again.'

★

Other mistakes occur when a secretary takes dictation a little too literally…

---

Dear Mr Blank,

Let's see. What shall I tell the boring old fool. Start – In reply to your letter of the twenty-seventh inst we are surprised to learn that the super-power two-ton used truck you purchased from us is not giving perfect satisfaction. We had to sell it quick before it fell to pieces, he was mug enough to buy it.

As you know, Mr Blank, we inspect all used vehicles thoroughly before turning them over to the purchaser. Your lorry was in perfect condition when it left our garage. That really is a very attractive dress you have on. New isn't it?

It is possible that your driver is at fault. Four miles to the gallon is very poor mileage for a vehicle in such good condition as yours. Four gallons to the mile would be about right. I never noticed you had a dimple just there before. It's a long time since we had a secretary with such outstanding attributes. Bring it round to our garage and we will have our expert mechanic make the proper adjustments. That'll do. Send it second class.

Yours sincerely,
Just sign it yourself.

---

## MEMO TO B.R.J.

I know you believe you understand what you think I said, but I am not sure you realise that what you heard is not what I meant.

P.J.C.

★

Unfortunately, the fact that the English language has so many words that sound alike, means that even the most efficient secretary can make mistakes when taking dictation:

'Some mothers I've seen are twenty foot around the middle.' (*Some others I've seen are twenty foot around the middle.*)

'The breeches are getting ancient.' (*The bridges are getting ancient.*)

'Where is the Spice centre?' (*Where is the Spy Centre?*)

'We require twenty-four each occasion.' (*We require twenty for each occasion.*)

★

**Postscript**

Did you hear about the absent-minded executive who came home, kissed his wife and started dictating a letter?

# PRIZE PUPILS

**'We are shut up in schools and college recitation rooms for ten or fifteen years, and come out at last with a bellyful of words and do not know a thing.'**
*Ralph Waldo Emerson* (1803-1882)

What nonsense! We learn a lot at school and college and university. What we learn may not make much sense, of course, but it can afford us a good deal of innocent pleasure. If proof is needed, here it is: a cornucopia of classic clangers culled from academic institutions around the English-speaking world...

'So Henry, with the help of Thomas Cromwell, set about dissolusioning the monastries.'

★

'The modern version of the astrolabe is the stethoscope.'

★

'A "shofar" is a person who drives a car for someone else.'

★

'Offa's Dyke was a church. Offa was a rather irrelevant king.'

★

'The thought of England coming under Spanish rule was unthinkable.'

★

'King Arthur, if he existed, would have been brave, noble and a little eccentric.'

★

'The natives of Macedonia did not believe, so Paul got stoned.'

★

'Coal-fire power stations should be built in the minefields.'

★

'Nuclear power stations are built at places on the coast, such as Luton.'

★

'If you try to cut through atoms, you get rough edges.'

★

'Henry VIII spent a long time on the throne trying to produce a strong male successor.'

★

'The second wife of Henry VIII was "Ann Berlin".'

★

'Florence Nightingale was a famous Swedish soprano.'

★

'Telepathy is a code invented by Morse.'

★

'Augustus remained in the same position for four years.'

★

'Thin silk used for ladies underwear is called Crepe Suzette.'

★

'Most of Falmouth's small peninsula is covered with water at all times, except the small section of the harbour.'

★

'Savonarola ruled Florence, not as he thought best, but how he thought it would be best ruled.'

★

'Because Wolsey failed to get the Pope his divorce, Henry dismissed him, and Wolsey died in 1530.'

★

'*Pot-pourri* is a French dish served in hot little pots.'

★

'Granite is an example of the type of rocks known as ingenius rocks, whereas limestone is a metaphoric rock.'

★

'An oxygen has eight sides.'

★

'*A priori* means first come first served.'

★

'Oedipus Complex was a famous queen of Egypt.'

★

'The Gorgons had long snakes in their hair and looked
like women only more horrible.'

'The Sewage canal is in Egypt.'

★

'Herrings swim about in the sea in shawls.'

★

'*Marseillaise* is a French salad dressing.'

★

'Electric volts are named after Voltaire, who invented
electricity.'

★

'The first commandment was when Eve told Adam to
eat the apple.'

★

'Pegasus is a hobby horse used by carpenters.'

★

'All people were petrified during the Stone Age.'

★

'An executive is a man who chops people's heads off.'

★

'When a man is married to one woman it is called
monotony.'

*

'The Pope lives in the Cacuum.'

*

'Mata Hari means suicide in Japanese.'

*

'Asperity is the drug from which asprins are made.'

*

'Abraham is in the Bible and is noted for his bosom.'

*

'A polygon is another name for a Mormon.'

*

'Blood consists of red corkscrews and white corkscrews.'

*

'When a woman has many husbands, it is called Pollyanna.'

*

'Garibaldi designed the Statue of Liberty.'

*

'Pidgin-English were pigeons used by the British to carry messages during the war.'

*

'The bowels are a, e, i, o, u, and sometimes w and y.'

*

'Abstinence makes the heart grow fonder.'

*

'Livid was a famous Roman poet.'

*

'Opium is a Chinese medicine discovered by Dr Fu Manchu.'

*

'Armadillic is the spanish navy defeated by the Duke of Wellington.'

*

'Insects is burned in some churches.'

*

'Zero was a Roman king who played the fiddle while Rome burned.'

★

'Saint Peter was a rabbit in a book by Beatrice Potter.'

★

'The earth resolves around the sun once a year.'

★

'Socrates died from an overdose of wedlock.'

★

'A blizzard is the inside of a chicken.'

★

'The mother of Abraham Lincoln died in infancy.'

★

'Equinox is a country near the Panama Canal.'

★

'Homer wrote a play called The Oddity.'

★

'Poetry is when every line starts with a capital letter.'

★

'Pasteur found a cure for rabbits.'

★

'Nicotine is the man who invented cigarettes.'

★

'In *Mrs Warren's Profession* her profession is the oldest profession, but she is not really a lost woman. She is just mislaid.'

★

'Columbine was the wife of the man who discovered America.'

★

'All strong men have good physics.'

★

'People who test your eyes are called optimists.'

★

'A palmist is someone who tells your fortune by looking in her crystal ball.'

★

'Parasites are people who live in Paris.'

★

'An aviary is a place where aviators sleep.'

'My sister has an allegory. If she eats strawberries she has the spots.'

★

'There are many types of eligable fish in the sea.'

★

'An Indian baby is called a caboose.'

★

'Reefs are what you put on coffins.'

★

'Henry VIII had an abbess on his knee and could not walk.'

★

'Handel was a little boy in a story by Grimm. He had a sister called Gristle.'

★

'It is sometimes difficult to hear what is being said in Church because the agnostics are so bad.'

★

'Ladies who sing two kinds of songs are called contraltos.'

★

'Rugby is a game played by men with odd shaped balls.'

★

'The liver is an infernal organ.'

★

'Moths eat hardly nothing, except holes.'

★

'Polonius is a sort of sausage.'

★

'Monsoon is a french word meaning Mister.'

★

'Karl Marx was the Marx brother who played the harp.'

★

'Kosher is Jewish pork.'

★

'Income is a yearly tax.'

★

'A centimeter is an insect with a hundred legs.'

★

'When a dog has puppies it is called a litre.'

★

'A doggerel is a little dog.'

★

'Cleopatra died because she was bitten on her asp.'

★

'The masculine of vixen is vicar.'

★

'Lady Godiva swam the English Channel.'

★

'Robinson Crusoe was a great operatic tenor.'

★

'Jesse Jones is the name of the locker where sailors go
when they drown.'

★

'Iran is the Bible of the Mohammedans.'

★

'A ruminating animal chews its cubs.'

★

'A fjord is a Norwegian car.'

★

'Gretna Green is a poison for killing rats.'

★

'The future of "I give" is "You take".'

★

'Philatelists were a race of people who lived in Biblical times.'

★

'Flora and Fauna were two siamese twins.'

★

' "After me, the deluge" was said by Noah when he raised the gang plank of the ark.'

★

'Conservation is when you talk to people.'

★

'There are a lot of currants in the sea.'

★

'A virgin forest is where the hand of man has never set foot.'

★

'Alma Mater was a famous opera singer.'

★

'Magnets are little creatures found in rotten apples.'

★

'*Pâté de foie gras* is an outdoor fair and circus held in New Orleans every year.'

★

'A commonplace is a busy corner in a town or village.'

★

'A mosquito is a child of black and white parents.'

★

'Flotsam and Jetsam were a famous team of coloured comedians.'

★

'Soviet is another name for a table napkin.'

★

'The smallest wind instrument is the Piccadilly.'

★

'Moll Flanders is the story of a Belgian gun girl.'

★

'In France even pheasants drink wine.'

★

'Euthenasia is the eastern part of Asia.'

★

'Naval Stores is where sailor's wives go shopping.'

★

'When a man has more than one wife he is a pigamist.'

★

'Belvedere is the name given to a male deer.'

★

'Shakespeare wrote tragedy, comedy and errors.'

★

'Autobiography is the history of motor cars.'

★

'People who live on the equator are called equestrians.'

★

'Ambiguity is telling the truth when you don't mean it.'

★

'Washington was a great general, he always had a fixed
determination to win or lose.'

★

' "I took thee for thy better": this is what Hamlet said
when he stabbed Polonius and thought he was a rat.'

★

'A hostage is a nice lady on an aeroplane.'

★

'A tambourine is a curved club which can be hurled so
that it will come back near the place from which it was
thrown.'

★

'In America some murderers are put to death by
electrolysis.'

★

'Jacob had a brother called See-saw.'

★

'Napoleon had three children, not one of which lived to
maternity.'

★

# QUICK MONEY

**'I am the very model of a modern Major-General, I've information vegetable, animal, and mineral.'**

*W.S. Gilbert* (1836-1911)

It is hard to believe I know, but even the military make mistakes. On the whole we don't hear about the blunders and bloomers of the armed forces because they are trained to keep that sort of thing under wraps. For example, take the case of the young corporal who hated the sight of his commanding officer. One evening at a party he was talking to a very attractive girl, when he saw the officer standing on the other side of the room.

'Do you know that ugly sap of an officer standing over there?' he said. 'He's the meanest bastard I've ever met.'

'Do you know who I am?' enquired the girl. 'I happen to be that officer's daughter.'

'Do you know who I am?' asked the corporal.

'No.'

'Thank the Lord for that.'

Risking the full-scale court martial (to say nothing of thorough investigation by MI5, MI6 and Chapman Pincher), here are my own favourite examples of uniformed confusion ...

Artillery Commander: 'Fire at will!'
Recruit: 'Where's Will?'

★

*Seen in a Ministry of Defence publication:*
'In Reference A, the cover letter at Reference B is an error. The additions at Annex B to Reference B are already incorporated in Annex A to Reference B, and

are those additional items per pack that will be required if the complete schedule at Annex A to Reference B are approved.'

★

In April 1945 a nineteen-year-old Japanese pilot made a big mistake. His great ambition was to die as a kamikaze pilot and he began to realise that ambition when he set off on his final mission surrounded by explosives. He should have aimed his aircraft at an American ship, but was slightly off target and instead he landed in the sea and was rescued by the US Navy.

The mistake meant that he lived.

★

*Notice in an army hospital:*
'Patients who are NCO's will wear their chevrons if marked "up" and if confined to bed will be pinned to the wall of the marquee above their i ̠ds.'

★

To disobey a command of a colonel is to invite disaster – at least that's the theory. One morning, on a tour of inspection, a colonel stopped at the kitchen of one of the companies in his command, where he met two men with a large soup kettle.

'Here you!' he bellowed. 'Run and fetch me a soup ladle and let me taste this.' Obeying orders, one of the men ran off and returned with a large ladle which he respectfully handed to the colonel.

The officer plunged the ladle into the pot, took a big mouthful of the steaming liquid and smacked his lips critically. He then let out one almighty shout that could be heard at GHQ half a mile away.

'Soup, you blasted fool, do you call that soup?' he roared.

'No, colonel, that's just some dish water we was carrying out.'

★

*Instructions from the Admiralty:*

'It is necessary for technical reasons that these warheads should be stored with the top at the bottom, and the bottom at the top. In order that there may be no doubt as to which is the top, and which is the bottom for storage purposes, it will be seen that the bottom of each has been labelled with the word TOP.'

*

A soldier in the parachute regiment was arrested by police when he landed in the middle of a four-lane highway in Illinois. The police charged him with not using an authorized entrance to a highway.

*

'What's the matter with you?' asked the major of a private who reported sick.

'I've got a pain in my abdomen', said the private.

'Your abdomen!' exclaimed the officer. 'You mean your stomach, my lad. Only second lieutenants have abdomens!'

*

*Army instructions:*

'Smoking is allowed as long as it does not interfere with the work, but when the DSO or any senior officers approach the station it would be as well if they were removed for the time being.'

*

*Company orders:*

'Any men wishing to make any alteration in their next-of-kin must send in a notification to Orderly Room by 8pm.'

*

The British Ministry of Defence built a concrete blockhouse in Scotland that turned out to be such an eyesore that when they had no further use for it in 1975 they had a problem as to how to sell it. It was made uglier by the fact that it had no windows, no doors and a flat roof. The following newspaper advertisement was drawn up to try to sell this architectural nightmare:

'For sale: Reinforced concrete eyesore. Would suit nervous spy or mushroom farmer with dangerous wife for whom outhouse with five foot walls ideal. Offers, suggestions, however inane, invited for monument to corrupted endeavour. Forest planting a condition of sale.'

*

## Postscript

Never make the fatal mistake of sounding too heroic. It might give the wrong impression...

'And there, son, you have the story of your dad during World War II.'

'Yes, dad, but why did you need all those other soldiers?'

*

# RECIPES FOR DISASTER

*'God sends meat, and the Devil sends cooks.'*
*English Proverb*

In Britain we love to see our menus written in French or Italian: it adds to the excitement and enjoyment of a meal out. We know that *pommes frites* are chips and *petit pois* are peas, but they sound so much more exotic in French. If you go abroad you'll find the British aren't the only ones who feel this way. Foreigners, too, like to print their menus in a language that isn't their own – and as often as not the language they choose is English. Unfortunately (if these real examples are anything to go by) the *haute cuisine* can lose some of its savour in translation ...

*From a café in Belgium*
**SNAX**
Hand and eeg
Pissoles and reas
Frightened eegs
Sauceage eeg and chaps
Battered cod peaces
\*\*\*
Cream Dognuts
Roast apple tart and source
Biscuit cease

————— ⋆ —————

*From a taverna in Sicily*
Hen Soop
Consumate
Mellon and prostitute hams

Mukroni of Niples
Spaghetti fungus

Satiated calamary
Kink prawns in butta
Red Mallet

Scallop vale of Milan
Dreaded Veal cutlets

Speciality of the hows: Young Dear Hunter
(Flash of young dear, objerjeans, muchrooms end
spaces, in wite whine sorts, all cocked up by your seat)

Raped carrots
Rise
Groin Salid
Chipped potatoz

Yogrot and gripes
Eyes creme

We recommend the cheez of the neighbour

Cofee Eggspress

Service not comprehended

———————— ★ ————————

*From a restaurant in Buenos Aires*
Testicles of Bull
Udder Milk Bag
Female calf intestine
Soft meat between Leather without bone
roasted at spit
Little Kids (Roasted or at spit)
Apple Pancake burned with Rum

———————— ★ ————————

*From a restaurant in Barcelona*
Pig Borshch
Cocked garlic with musturd sauce
Liver Offal with stuffed

Marooned Duchess and Braised surprise

Bruined squid with pee
Baked Cheese fingers
Roasted Haddock Fish

Cucumber Pudding
Apple Crumbs
Live fruit
Rhubarb and Prune surprise
Many cheese

———— ★ ————

*From a Swedish hotel*
Tongue Loaf with leaves
Venison parcel
Surprised chicken
Cracked pudding (Biled)
Salami stuff roll
Rice Hashed
Mucked Shrimp

———— ★ ————

*From a Spanish restaurant*
Fizz soop
Whores Dover (mixed)
Boled eegs in creme source
*

Rost cock
Spited hen
Buff stek
Hambugger
*

Backed beas
Potato chops
Cabitch
*

Rice sputnik
Pankasies
Pankasies with bebber and jem
*

Lemon jews
*

Turkey coffee
'Enjoy to eat now, always bring back after.'
Local mutto

———————— ★ ————————

*From a luxury hotel in Cairo*
Soap of the day
Hard egg with sauce mayonnaise
Prawn cock and tail
Frog leagues
*

Muscles of Marines
Lobster thermos
Fresh caut soul
*

Two peasants
Larks in the spit
Wild duck in orang sorts
*

Cock in wine
Lioness cutlet
Steak O'Poivre
Biftek Gordon Blue
Iris Stew a L'Ecossaise
*

French beas
French fried ships
Spineitch
Sprouts of Bruxelles
*

Please to try the tarts of the house,
available for your delight on the trolley.
Cheese and biskiss
Cafe au lit
If you are wishing to show feelings, wait untill you see
the manageress.

———————— ★ ————————

# SIGNS OF THE TIMES

'Can ye not discern the signs of the times?' asked the poet.

Well, yes … and here are my favourites:

*Sign seen on an electricity pylon:*
**DANGER!**
To touch these wires will result in instant death. Anyone found doing so will be severely prosecuted.

★

*Notice on the edge of a lake in Cumbria:*
**ANY PERSON PASSING BEYOND THIS POINT WILL BE DROWNED**
By Order of the Magistrates

★

*Sign seen in Merseyside*
**LIVERPOOL MATERNITY HOSPITAL**
(Not Accident)

★

In a cemetery in Pennsylvania there is a sign which says:
**PERSONS ARE PROHIBITED FROM PICKING FLOWERS FROM ANY BUT THEIR OWN GRAVES.**

★

In a large park in Ohio there is a small bandstand, around which are many seats. A sign states:
'The seats in this vicinity of the bandstand are for the use of ladies. Gentlemen should make use of them only after the former are seated.'

★

In a provincial English theatre there is a sign on the wall, unfortunately positioned right by the public lavatories:
'Patrons are requested to remain seated throughout the entire performance.'

★

*From a school in Derbyshire:*

'WILL THE INDIVIDUAL WHO BORROWED A LADDER FROM THE CARETAKER LAST MONTH KINDLY RETURN SAME IMMEDIATELY, OTHERWISE FURTHER STEPS WILL BE TAKEN.'

★

*From a garage in Hertfordshire:*

'Please do not smoke near the pumps. If your life isn't worth anything – petrol is!'

★

*Spotted recently near Colchester:*

'GO SLOW – CONCEALED ROAD ENTRANCE – NO OVERTAKING FOR THE NEXT 200 YRS.'

★

*This sign was seen on the gate of a farm in Kentucky:*

NOTIS

'Trespassers will be percecuted to the full extent of two mongrel dogs which aint never been too sociable with strangers and one dubble br'l shotgun which aint loaded with sofa pillows. DAM if I aint gittin tired of this hell raisin round my place.'

★

*A farmer in Norfolk put up a similar warning, but he was a little more direct:*

'Trespassers beware! I shoot every tenth trespasser. The ninth one just left.'

★

*On the Thames near Henley:*

'DANGER – When red flags are flying flooding of the river is imminent and members of the public must not leave the river banks.'

★

*Sign seen in a small repair shop:*

NO CREDIT

(Sad stories of three delinquents)

One said: 'I'll pay you if I live.'

He died.
One said: 'I'll see you tomorrow.'
He went blind.
One said: 'I'll pay you or go to hell.'
He must have gone.

*From a farm in Sussex:*
'DOGS FOUND WORRYING WILL BE SHOT.'

★

*Found in a public garden in Cornwall:*
'No person shall walk, run, stand, sit or lie on the grass
in this pleasure ground.'

★

*Seen in a London department store:*
'BARGAIN BASEMENT UPSTAIRS.'

★

*Notice seen in the vicinity of Victoria Station:*
'Closed for official opening.'

★

# TRANSLATION PLEASE

**Belinda: Ay, but you know we must return good for evil.**
**Lady Brute: That may be a mistake in the translation.**
*Sir John Vanbrugh* (1664-1726)

There has never been a foreign phrase book quite like
this one – but each of the incredible mistranslations that
follow has appeared in a real phrase book at one time or
another. I have simply brought them all together in the
hope of furthering the cause of international understanding …

| | |
|---|---|
| *à bientôt* | just a little drop |
| *abito* | a piece of |
| *ab imo* | it belongs to him |
| *achtung* | my mouth hurts |
| *à bras ouverts* | an empty brassiere |
| *ad hoc* | the wine is finished |
| *acme* | spots |
| *actum ne ageas* | it's been a long time |
| *affaire de coeur* | pigeon bazaar |
| *a fortiori* | he hit me |
| *agape* | a big hole |
| *ahorros* | a four-legged animal used for racing |
| *aide de camp* | an effeminate servant |
| *à la russe* | in a hurry |
| *à la carte* | served from the trolley |
| *amazon* | quite surprising |
| *amour propre* | dock pile |
| *Angebot* | to wait, loiter |
| *annus* | behind |
| *apenas* | joy, pleasure |
| *apéritif* | dentures |
| *à propos* | a potty under the bed |

| | |
|---|---|
| *arcadia* | amusements |
| *artichaut* | sneeze |
| *ars longa* | big posterior |
| *auspuff* | cobweb duster |
| *autofahrt* | backfire |
| | |
| *bacchich* | backache |
| *bagatelle* | talkative female |
| *battre le pavé* | thump the pavement |
| *beau geste* | big joke |
| *bien* | French vegetable |
| *bombe* | explosive |
| *bonis avibus* | free ride on public transport |
| *bonhomme* | very gay |
| *bon ton* | large heap |
| *brouhaha* | French joy of cooking |
| *brefs* | pants |
| | |
| *ça ira* | pardon? |
| *caffe Nero* | coffee served with burning brandy |
| *ça ne fait rien* | the weather is fine |
| *carte blanche* | a white barrow |
| *cercle privé* | around the toilet |
| *c'est la vie* | this is the way |
| *c'est magnifique* | it is very large, enormous |
| *chagrin* | cleaning lady's smile |
| *château* | French conversation |
| *compos mentis* | his brain is rotting |
| *congé* | a dance |
| *coq d'or* | entrance to the gents |
| *corpus* | dead body |
| *cortège* | small house in the country |
| *coup* | hen house |
| *crèche* | sound of breaking crockery |
| *cul-de-sac* | out of the bag |
| *cum priviligio* | he had the honour of her company |

110

| | |
|---|---|
| *damnosa* | very inquisitive |
| *de gustibus* | very windy |
| *déjeuner* | travel |
| *déjà vu* | nice to see you |
| *demosthenic* | fan of a Greek singer |
| *de mal en pis* | urgent need to pass water |
| *de pis en pis* | from bad to worse |
| *de optimo maximo* | very good eyesight |
| *déshabiller* | kick the habit |
| *désolé* | a fish |
| | |
| *ecrasez l'infame* | a madman is after me |
| *eg* | egg |
| *enosis* | he's very clever |
| *emeraudes* | piles |
| *en ami* | hostile person |
| *en arrière* | suppository |
| *entourloupette* | the insane are on holiday |
| *entrée* | in a mess |
| *eureka!* | unpleasant odour |
| *extrados* | more please |
| | |
| *faggotto* | cigarette |
| *farceur* | comic play |
| *farci* | farce |
| *faux pas* | don't do it! |
| *fille de joie* | very happy |
| *fiasco* | Italian white wine |
| *flèche* | skin |
| *fruits de mer* | sea weed |
| | |
| *galimafrée* | madam, I am unattached |
| *gendarme* | the strong arm of the law |
| *grande dame* | fat lady |
| *grand prix* | large reward |
| *gurke* | breaking wind |
| | |
| *hasta la vista* | you have nice views |

| | |
|---|---|
| *hic sepultus* | indigestion |
| *homme d'affaires* | libertine |
| *homo sapiens* | consenting adult |
| *hors concours* | horse chestnut |
| *hors de combat* | dog fight |
| *horloge* | brothel |
| *humani generis* | generous people |
| | |
| *imo pectore* | he kissed her |
| *in toto* | wearing a ballet skirt |
| *infra dig* | archaeologist |
| *in loco parentis* | in one's parent's train |
| *in statu pupillari* | contact lens |
| *inter alia* | domestic fights |
| *intermezzo* | between meals |
| *intime* | at the right moment |
| | |
| *jeu de mots* | I've got the moth |
| *jus contra bellum* | I am overweight |
| *juste milieu* | just a minute! |
| *juvenalia* | adolescent |
| | |
| *karat* | a vegetable |
| *kip* | chicken |
| *kipper* | bantam |
| *krebbs* | crabs |
| | |
| *laissez faire* | lazy woman |
| *lapsus memoriae* | poor memory |
| *lampone* | raspberry |
| *largo* | Italian beer |
| *legato* | tailor's measurement |
| *lemma* | fruit drink |
| *libido* | bathroom fitting |
| *lite pendente* | fine necklace |
| *lingua franco* | speaking your mind |
| *l'état c'est moi* | I am in a state |
| *lieu* | lavatory |

| | |
|---|---|
| *loc. cit.* | there is a lock on the door |
| *ma foi* | my liver |
| *magnum cum laude* | you'll have to turn the volume up |
| *maladie* | madam |
| *mal vu* | poor eyesight |
| *manqué* | nasty |
| *mauvais goût* | a swollen leg |
| *mise en page* | a slip of the pen |
| *mistral* | folk singer |
| *negligé* | negligent |
| *n'importe* | there is no port left |
| *noblesse oblige* | nobody will help |
| *nom de plume* | quill pen |
| *nouvelle vague* | a modern novel |
| *obiit* | get out! |
| *objet de virtue* | prostitute |
| *obscurum per obscuris* | you're standing in front of the light |
| *odium* | a drug |
| *odium theologicum* | incense |
| *omphallus* | large symbol |
| *O si sic omnes* | illness in lap due to rocking motion of boat |
| *palomine* | friend of mine |
| *par excellence* | very good father |
| *pax Britannica* | British fathers |
| *pas de deux* | father of twins |
| *passé* | father has spoken |
| *per annum* | laxatives |
| *piano* | shipping line |
| *pinxit* | elf |
| *pis aller* | open sewer |

113

| | |
|---|---|
| *pizzicato* | small pizza |
| *polonaise* | hay fever |
| *presto* | tight shoe |
| | |
| *quadrille* | dance for squares |
| *quod erat demonstrandum* | demonstration by pest control officer |
| | |
| *rechauffé* | rearrange |
| *rentier* | give money to landlord |
| *rites de passage* | constipation |
| | |
| *sang froid* | black pudding |
| *semper paratus* | always a parrot |
| *son et lumière* | your son is alight |
| *sotto voce* | slurred speech |
| | |
| *table d'hôte* | hot plate |
| *tant pis* | dipsomaniac relative |
| *tartine* | waitress |
| *touché* | slightly mad |
| *terra cotta* | fear of beds |
| *tertium quid* | £3.00 |
| *tour de force* | troop inspection |
| *tour de main* | palmistry |
| *typhoon* | milllionaire |
| | |
| *vi et armis* | a small army |
| *vice versa* | limerick |
| *vis-à-vis* | to return the insult |
| *voltarsi* | leap-frog |
| *volte face* | wooden horse |
| *viz* | face |
| | |
| *yarmulke* | here is your milk |
| *yashmak* | raincoat |
| | |
| *zweifellos* | two men |

# UNHOLY WRIT

**'There are three sexes – men, women, and clergymen.'**
*Sydney Smith* (1771-1845)

Yes, the clergy *do* make mistakes now and again, and – heavens above! – there are even errors in the Bible. God moves in a wondrous way his mysteries to perform …

*A vicar announced in his parish magazine:*
'Prebendary Brinsley-Smythe will be preaching at St Margaret's on Sunday, 14 May, and my colleague the Right Rev. Arnold Dean on Sunday, 21 May. On both these Sundays I hope to be away on holiday.'

*

*From a parish newsletter in Birmingham:*
'In the Parish Hall on Sunday 6 April, The Devil.'

*

The Rev. Edgar Dodson, of Campden, chose as his theme for his sermon one Sunday the commandment *Thou shalt not steal*. During the service someone stole his car.

*

*From a parish newsletter in Beaulieu, Hampshire:*
'There will be a procession next Sunday afternoon in the grounds of the monastery, but if it rains in the afternoon the procession will take place in the morning.'

*

*From the Order of Service, St Jude's, Ramsgate:*
'Hymn … No. 385
    (Congregation standing)
Sermon: "What are you standing for:" '

*

*From a church notice board in Leamington Spa:*
'Anyone having relatives buried in the churchyard is asked to be so good as to keep them in order.'

★

*From a parish newsletter in Bromsgrove:*
'A special service of thanksgiving for the success of the recent campaign in aid of distressed daughters of the clergy will be held at 6pm and will be followed by mating in the Church Hall.'

★

*From a church magazine in Hull:*
'We are sorry to announce that Mr Albert Brown has been quite unwell, owing to his recent death, and is taking a short holiday to convalesce.'

★

*Seen outside a small chapel in Gwent:*
'DON'T LET WORRY KILL YOU OFF – LET THE CHURCH HELP'

★

*Sign outside a church in Wandsworth:*
'Earth's last war. How and wear will it be fought? At Adventist Church, Sunday evening.'

★

*Notice outside a chapel in Swansea:*
'THE PREACHER NEXT SUNDAY EVENING WILL BE THE REV. HUBERT THOMPSON, AFTER WHICH THE CHAPEL WILL BE CLOSED FOR 3 WEEKS FOR REPAIRS.'

★

*Sign seen hanging on a church door in Staffordshire:*
'This is the gate of heaven enter ye all by this door. (This door kept locked because of draught, use back entrance.)'

★

An edition of the Bible printed in London in 1631 had to be withdrawn from circulation, owing to a typographical error. One vital word had been missed out of the Seventh Commandment. It read: 'Thou shalt commit adultery.'

★

A Bible published in 1568 and now known as the 'Treacle Bible' contained a slip that was corrected in subsequent editions. The correction read: 'Note that the line: "Is there no treacle in Gilead?" should read: "Is there no balm in Gilead?" '

*

Infuriated that no one answered the front door to him (when he was sure the household was at home) the vicar left his visiting card, having written on it: 'Revelations 3:20'. ('Behold I stand at the door and knock: if anyone hears my voice and opens the door I will come to him')

The following Sunday, as the congregation were leaving, a lady parishioner handed him her card, which bore the inscription: 'Genesis 3:10'. ('I heard the sound of thee in the garden and I was afraid, because I was naked and hid myself')

*

A clergyman was telling his congregation of the effects of drink, and said: 'I hope the time will soon come when all liquor will be poured into the river. Now let us sing hymn number 162.' Unfortunately the title of hymn 162 was: *Shall we Gather at the River*?

*

A bishop was overheard whispering to a fellow member of the cloth, who seemed considerably the worse for drink, 'I Corinthians 10:12.' ('Wherefore let him that thinketh he standeth take heed lest he fall')

*

*Correction to a biblical misprint:*
Note that in John 15:13, 'wife' should read 'life'. Thus correcting: 'Greater love hath no man than this, that a man lay down his wife for his friends.'

*

A bishop had been speaking with some feeling about the use of cosmetics by girls.
'The more experience I have of lipstick', he declared, 'the more distasteful I find it.'

A bishop received the following note from the vicar of a village in his diocese:

'My Lord, I regret to inform you of the death of my wife. Can you possibly send me a substitute for the weekend?'

*

While sailing back to port after taking part in anti-submarine exercises, the captain of a British destroyer sent a signal to his fellow commander on board a submarine asking if he was becoming bored with always acting as the target. The reply was: 'Hebrews 13:8'. ('Jesus Christ the same yesterday, and today, and forever')

*

Charles Lamb was in the habit of wearing a white cravat, and was often mistaken for a clergyman. At a dinner, among a large number of guests his cravat caused the usual mistake and he was asked to say grace. Looking up and down the table he said: 'Is there no cl-cl-clergyman present?'

'No, Sir' answered a guest.

'Then', said Lamb, bowing his head, 'Let us thank the Lord.'

*

# VARIETY AND SPICE

'A celebrity is a person who works hard all his life to become known, then wears dark glasses to avoid being recognised.'

*Fred Allen*

When it comes to making mistakes, there really is no business like show business. Some of the gaffes of the great and famous are merely ghastly – Larry Hagman forgetting his words at a Royal Variety Show, James Mason forgetting the names of the ballet dancers he was introducing at another Royal Variety Show. But others have their comic sides ...

\*

Harry Secombe was invited to perform before the inmates of Pentonville Prison. The concert went very well until he sang his famous rendition of *Bless This House*, which was slightly unfortunate as it contains the words: 'Bless these walls so firm and stout, keeping want and trouble out...'

\*

As he readily admits, Dickie Henderson is not beyond putting his dainty feet into things. He once found himself at a tedious show-business gathering, where a woman who had a dreadful singing voice was attempting to entertain. He turned to the man next to him to express his opinion of the singer, saying how dreadful he considered she was.

'That is my wife' explained the man.

To cover up his embarrassment, Dickie said:

'Well, it's not her fault. The song is terrible.' – which was unfortunate. The man had written the song.

\*

Two of the BBC's most respected – and reliable – commentators are Brian Johnston and John Snagge, but even they are not immune from the occasional slip of the tongue. During a cricket match Johnston had meant to say of a player:
'He's sticking out his bottom – like someone sitting on a shooting stick.' Unfortunately he got his words mixed up and came out with a quite unprintable spoonerism. On another occasion he claimed that cricketer Ray Illingworth 'is just relieving himself at the Pavilion End.'

And it was John Snagge, who, in a frenzy at the end of the Oxford and Cambridge Boat Race, exclaimed: 'I don't know who is in the lead … it's either Oxford or Cambridge.'

★

David Hamilton made a bit of a bloomer one evening while acting as a television announcer. Before he went on the air, he dropped his script and on bending down to pick it up, his trousers split. As he had another engagement later that evening, the trousers had to be whisked away for repairs and David was forced to face the cameras in his underpants. Viewers at home watched oblivious of the fact that if the camera had dropped just a couple of inches they would have seen more of David than they had bargained for.

*

The boxer Henry Cooper once made a mistake over an after-dinner speech. It wasn't that he forgot his speech, the problem was that he forgot the dinner. He was sitting at home watching television when he received a telephone call telling him where he should be. He arrived just in time to give his speech.

*

A well-known actress, who, for obvious reasons, wishes to remain anonymous, was once giving a cocktail party and had had just a little too much to drink. Halfway through the party she saw three guests coming towards her. She assumed they were leaving because they were wearing their coats, but actually they had just arrived. Staggering up to them she said:
'Oh, must you really stay? Can't you go?'

*

Big-hearted Arthur Askey once made a little blunder when appearing in a show with Danny La Rue and Carole Channing. After he had come off stage, he saw Danny La Rue in full drag bending over, so for a bit of fun Arther tip-toed over and pinched his bottom shouting 'Wotcher cock!' To his great embarrassment, it was not Danny La Rue at all, but Carole Channing.

*

*Coronation Street* star Pat Phoenix does not usually have a bad memory for names and faces, but once at the television studios she was greeted by a woman who said, 'How nice to see you again.' Pat hadn't a clue who the woman was so she smiled and said 'Hello'. The woman continued 'er ... I'm Mary Wilson'. So Pat said 'How nice' and turned away. It was not until about ten minutes later that she realised that it was the poetess wife of the then Prime Minister, Harold Wilson.

The impresario, Lew Grade, once saw a double-act in a show which he thought had great potential. After the performance he went backstage to congratulate the performers and to try to sign them up, saying that he would turn them into big stars, and promising to double their money. He enquired who their current agent was.

'A man called Lew Grade', they replied.

*

Quiz-master Nicholas Parsons was once hosting a charity fashion show, where the models weren't professionals but local housewives. Nicholas is a master of 'pretend' languages: he gabbles away in gobbledy-gook but can make it sound like French, or German. He interviewed each of the models in turn and discovered that one of the girls was born in West Germany, so for a laugh, he began describing her attire in his own unique German. The woman became very upset, and claimed that he was being very vulgar and insulting her – in German!

*

Sadly, history does not relate the name of the restaurant bandleader who made the mistake of sending a note over to the table where the playwright George Bernard Shaw was having dinner. The anonymous bandleader asked if there was anything Mr Shaw would like the band to play.

'Yes', came the reply. 'Dominoes.'

*

# WINDOW DRESSING

'Advertisements are now so numerous that they are very negligently perused, and it is therefore become necessary to gain attention by magnificence of promises, and by eloquences and sometimes sublime and sometimes pathetic.'

*Samuel Johnson* (1709-84)

The 'eloquences' here are all sublime – advertisements, notices, signs, announcements, spotted in shop windows here, there and everywhere...

'EARS PIERCED WHILE YOU WAIT.'

*

An electrical shop in West Bromwich with a special offer on washing machines has the following notice in the window: 'Don't kill your wife. Let our washing machines do the dirty work.'

*

*Notice seen in a Sunderland chemists:*
'WE DISPENSE WITH ACCURACY.'

*

'If you are willing to pay just a little more and are looking for a really fascinating out-of-the-ordinary pet, may we suggest you try the second floor and ask to see our Miss Burley.'

*

*Seen in a shop window in New Delhi:*
'The company will not be liable for any loss or damage caused by fire, Acts of God, or any other public enemies of the government.'

*

'The Chancellor of the Exchequer will speak at the Conservative Club Garden Party. Beware of pickpockets.'

'Model required – willing to pose for nude artist.'

*

'PIANO LESSONS – SPECIAL PAINS GIVEN
TO BEGINNERS.'

*

'Why go anywhere else and be cheated when you can
come here?'

*

'WE EXCHANGE EVERYTHING. BICYCLES,
WASHING MACHINES, ETC., BRING YOUR
WIFE AND GET THE DEAL OF YOUR LIFE.'

*

'Try our superior butter. Nobody can touch it.'

*

*Sign seen in a local dairy:*
'YOU CAN'T BEAT OUR MILK, BUT YOU CAN
WHIP OUR CREAM.'

★

*Sign seen in the window of a Hawaiian dress shop:*
'You will never find better or more exciting bikinis than ours – they are simply the tops!'

★

'FOR SALE: Kenwood mixer, large size, with all attachments, including tooth extractor.'

★

'The Electrical Contractors' Association will be holding their annual conference here on Monday night. The discussion will be followed by a light lunch.'

★

*Sign in the window of a New York butcher, presumably appealing to the more humane members of the community:*
'PORK SAUSAGES FROM PIGS THAT DIED HAPPY.'

★

'GENTLEMEN TAKEN AND DONE FOR.'

★

'LOST: 4 single pound notes, 14 March, in the vicinity of Market Street. Of sentimental value. Reward.'

★

'Dr Anderson, who is a leading authority on this important subject, will speak on the general questions of weed control, and Miss Trueman will follow with a short talk on the control of wild oats of which she has made a special study.'

★

'OUR MOTTO IS TO GIVE OUR CUSTOMERS THE VERY LOWEST PRICES AND WORK-MANSHIP.'

★

'Customers leaving garments longer than 30 days will now be disposed of.'

★

'BOAT FOR SALE: ONLY ONE OWNER. GREEN IN COLOUR.'

★

'Every Thursday we offer all old age pensioners a free soap, bleach and dry, plus hot steam press to make anything you may have like new.'

★

'For Sale: 1 Chaste long and other bits and pieces.'

★

'THE MANAGEMENT RESERVE THE RIGHT TO REMOVE ANY WOMAN THEY CONSIDER IMPROPER.'

★

'Gone to lunch – if not back by five then out to dinner also.'

★

'LOST A WHITE BEAGLE DOG WITH BROWN HEAD ON NORTH END ROAD.'

★

*A sign in a Los Angeles sports shop boasts:*
'We sell everything a golfer uses except profanity, and if you use our goods you won't need that.'

★

'FOR SALE: 1968 Morris Minor. A good running car, completely re-sprayed with new engine. This will not last long.'

★

'WASH AND SET, special offer: we will blow dry pensioners free on early closing day.'

★

'OSCAR'S FUNERAL PARLOUR – the service with a smile.'

★

'LOST at the meat market – bloodhound.'

★

*The following notice was seen in the window of a Suffolk farmhouse:*
'HORSE MANURE FOR SALE. BRING YOUR OWN BUCKET.'

★

'WANTED – MAN TO WASH DISHES AND TWO
WAITRESSES.'

RIP!

---

'Same Day Cleaners – 48-Hour Service. We do not tear your clothes with machinery. We do it carefully by hand.'

---

'MONDAY 6.30pm. "What is Hell?" Tip-up seats. Everyone will be welcome to join us.'

---

'Urgently needed, a woman to sew buttons on the fourth floor.'

---

'Customers who consider our waiters uncivil should see the manageress.'

---

'SATURDAY NIGHT DISCO – VERY EXCLUSIVE – EVERYBODY WELCOME'

---

*Outside the roller-disco the sign said:*
'Come in your thousands! The hall holds 500.'

---

*A Women's Institute displayed the following in their window:*
'The Evening of clairvoyance on Thursday 26 November, at 7.00pm has been cancelled owing to unforeseen circumstances.'

---

# XPLAIN YOURSELF

*Medical Officer:* How are your bowels working?
*Recruit:* Haven't been issued with any sir.
*M.O.:* I mean, are you constipated?
*Recruit:* No, sir, I volunteered.
*M.O.:* Heavens, man, don't you know the King's English?
*Recruit:* No, sir, is he?

Sometimes, it's not what we say but the way that we say it that leads us into troubled waters. Can you work out what each of these sentences is about? They have been transcribed just as I heard them – with rough translations underneath.

'Weev gorra gerrus imbux.'
   (We've got to get our hymn books.)

★

'Astle clowt thee if tha dunt gioer.'
   (I shall hit you if you do not stop.)

★

'Eesezitin tis burraberritiz.'
   (He says it is not his but I bet it is.)

★

'Anteldim burreewunt lissen.'
   (I told him but he would not listen.)

★

'Sumatsupeer.'
   (Something seems to be wrong.)

★

'Shut thigob.'
   (Will you please be quiet.)

★

'Asta gorrit withee?'
   (Did you happen to bring it with you?)

★

'Middadsez yegorra shurrup.'
  (My father says will you please be quiet.)

★

'Lerrus gerrus puddindanus.'
  (Let us eat our dessert now.)

★

'Astha gorrit reight?'
  (Are you sure you are correct?)

★

English spoken with a regional accent has a charm of its own, though to my mind the only people who manage to make English sound positively sexy are the French. Here, *par exemple*, is a Frenchman's account of the Fall of Adam from the Garden of Eden:

'Monsieur Adam, he vake up – he sees une belle demoiselle aslip in ze garden. Voila de la chance! "Bonjour, Madame Iv." Madame Iv, she vake; she holeher fan before to her face. Adam put on his eye-glass to admire ze tableau, and zey make von promenade. Madame Iv, she feel hungry. She see appel on ze arbre. Serpent se promène sur l'arbre – make one walk on ze tree. "Monsieur le Serpent", says Iv, "vill you not have ze bonté to pick me some appel? J'ai faim." "Certainement, Madame Iv, charme de vous voir." "Holà mon ami, ar-r-rêtez-vous," say Adam – "Stop! Stop! que songez vous faire? Was madness is zees? You must not pick ze appel!" Ze snake, he take one pinch of shnuff, he say: "Au, Monsieur Adam, do you not know how zere is nossing proheebet ze ladies? Madame Iv, permit me to offer you some of zeese fruit defendu – zeese forbidden fruit." Iv, she make one courtesy – ze snake, he fill her parasol wiz ze appel. He says: "Monsieur Adam, he will eat ze appel, but you, Madame Iv, cannot become more of a goddess zan you are now." An' zat feenish Madame Iv.'

★

130

## Postscript

Of course, English doesn't have to be spoken in an outlandish accent to become utterly incomprehensible. Here is the wording of a proposed amendment to a Standing Order that was put before parliament not long ago – and written in impeccable English:

'In the Nuts (unground) (other than ground nuts) Order, the expression nuts shall have reference to such nuts, other than ground nuts, as would but for this amending order not qualify as nuts (unground) (other than ground nuts) by reason of their being nuts (unground).'

# YOU SAID *WHAT*?

'The old weather-beaten she-dragon who guards you.'
said of Mrs Malaprop in 'The Rivals' by
*R.B. Sheridan* (1751-1816)

In 1775 the playwright, Richard Brinsley Sheridan, created one of the most enduring of all comic characters – the immortal Mrs Malaprop. This wonderful woman had the habit of continually confusing words that have similar sounds but no similarity in meaning, and has given her name to this amusing practice. The 'malapropism' is a comic device still used today – intentionally by comediennes such as Hylda Baker ('Just what are you incinerating?') and Hilda Ogden ('We've got a lovely murial on the wall'), and unintentionally by members of the general public: A woman went to her local GP and asked him for some 'contradiction pills'. He said: 'Madam, you're ignorant!' 'Yes, I know, six months', she replied.

Here are some of the *original* malapropisms created by Sheridan for his Mrs M:

'Illiterate him, I say, from your memory.'

★

'He is the very pine-apple of politeness.'

★

'It gives me the hydrostatics to such a degree.'

★

'She's as headstrong as an allegory on the banks of the Nile.'

★

'If I reprehend anything in this world, it is the use of my oracular tongue, and a nice derangement of epitaphs.'

★

'I own the soft impeachment.'

★

Having read the *Book of Mistaikes* this far, you'll not be surprised to learn that to call malapropisms 'malapropisms' is itself a mistake! It implies that Mrs Malaprop was the first to use them. They should really be called Dogberryisms, for it was William Shakespeare in *Much Ado About Nothing* who caused Constable Dogberry to utter so-called 'malapropisms', two centuries before Mrs Malaprop was born!

*Dogberry:* You are thought here to be the most senseless and fit man for the constable of the watch, therefore bear you the lantern. This is your charge: you shall comprehend all vagrom men: you are bid any man to stand, in the prince's name.
*Watch:* How if a'will not stand?
*Dogberry:* Why, then, take no note of him, but let him go: and presently call the rest of the watch together, and thank God you are rid of a knave ... You shall also make no noise in the streets; for, for the watch to babble and to talk is most tolerable and not to be endured.

Four hundred years after the creation of Dogberry you can still here the most outrageous and grotesque misapplications of words in everyday situations. Hear are some of the ones I've picked up:

'We were able to see right into the Royal disclosure.'

★

'He's got an allegory to kissing – it's a detergent to his love life.'

★

'My sister used massacre on her eyes.'

★

'We used to play cowboys and indians and I was your squawk.'

★

'I'm having the kitchen work surfaces covered with formosa.'

133

★

'My son's bringing his finance home. They're getting married soon.'

★

'My father is retarded on a pension.'

★

'We're going to make some thermostat copies of this letter.'

★

'He works in an incinerator where they burn the refuge.'

★

'I think those phonographic films are disgusting.'

★

'It happened during the French resolution.'

★

'My doctor gave me a conscription for some medicine.'

★

'My daughter is three months stagnant.'

★

'He had to use biceps to deliver the baby.'

★

'My husband is a marvellous lover. He knows all my erroneous zones.'

★

'I was so surprised you could have knocked me down with a fender.'

★

'My husband communicates to work daily on the train.'

★

'That was before he was erected as Prime Minister.'

★

# ZIZZ IZ ZE END

When the publishers approached me to compile this book they gave me a very clear brief. 'What we want', they said, 'is an amazing mixture of misprints, mistakes and misunderstandings, a collection of classic clangers, hilarious howlers and headlines gone haywire, a devastating dictionary of disaster from the dreadful (the true case of the car delivered without a steering wheel) to the delightful (the true case of the wig that didn't get to Lady Godiva's pageant in time).'

Well, if I'm not very much mistaken (and, under the circumstances, it doesn't much matter if I am) they've got what they asked for – *except* for the 'true case' of the car delivered without a steering wheel and the 'true case' of Lady Godiva's missing wig. I would have loved to have included both those stories, but having investigated them I find they're not true at all!

Believe it or not, all the mistakes in this book are real ones. I've not included any unless I felt they were genuine – so if you're disappointed that I haven't featured your favourite story of the airline pilot who mistakenly flew to New York instead of New Delhi because his plane was facing the wrong direction at Heathrow (or the one about the day the fire alarm at a concert hall caused the Boston Symphony Orchestra to be drenched while playing Handel's Water Music), rest assured that you can go on telling the stories, but I couldn't, since ruthless investigative journalism had shown them to be apocryphal.

Of the scores of true-life mishaps I've learnt about in the course of my researches, these last twenty are my favourites. None of them is of epic proportions and that's why I like them. It's the small-scale calamities like these that serve to remind us that when we get up tomorrow morning we may well be able to lose our tragic awareness for an hour or two, but we shall desperately need our sense of the comic ...

In March 1977, police in Dover, Kent, were contacted by an hysterical woman who had just seen a car driving along at great speed with a body sticking out of the boot. Fortunately she had the presence of mind to take down the car's number and in a matter of minutes the police were able to trace it. Sure enough there were two legs sticking out of the boot. They stopped the car and were about to arrest the driver when the 'body' climbed out of the boot. He was a garage mechanic who was listening for a rattling noise that only occurred when the car was in motion.

*

A couple from Enfield, Middlesex, were sent to Singapore on a two year assignment. Because they were going to be away for so long they decided to take their pet poodle, Dolores, with them. Not long after their arrival they went out to a restaurant for lunch, taking Dolores with them. Not being able to speak the language they had to use sign language to show that they wished the dog to have something to eat as well. The waiter appeared to understand and Dolores was led off happily into the kitchen. The couple tucked into their first course expecting the dog to be brought back any minute, but it returned about half-an-hour later – as the centrepiece of their meal.

*

In America a brand new cookery book appeared on the market with a delicious recipe for Caramel Slices. It was a very easy recipe, the main ingredient being a can of condensed milk which, the book said, you put into a pot and heated for four hours. The book omitted to say anything about putting water in the pot too – and without water the can would explode.

Every copy of the book had to be recalled, making it one of the most expensive cookery books ever produced.

136

The book reads: MAKE YOUR PARTY GO WITH A BANG

*

In 1932 a couple went shopping in London. It was close to Christmas and they visited all the large West End stores. At the end of the day they returned home by taxi, loaded down with large parcels. Back home they discovered that they seemed to have one package that neither of them remembered purchasing, and to their astonishment, on opening it they discovered it was a jewellery box filled with diamonds and rubies and hundreds of precious stones. They immediately took it to the nearest police station, and the jewels were later valued at over £250,000 – several million pounds by today's standards. Surprisingly enough nobody claimed them, though the police eventually traced their owner, a Russian Grand Duchess. The jewels had been part of the Russian Crown Jewels, and no one noticed when they went missing.

*

In February 1981, dustman Brian Brooks opened his garage door expecting to see the £700 worth of property that he had stored there – two electric motors, a washing machine, a television set, a sun lounger, a work bench, car jacks, ramps and various tools. Instead he found it completely empty. Local council workmen had been along, cleared the garage and allocated it to someone else. A mistake was made over the garage numbering and the council had emptied the *wrong* garage! Unfortunately the council had since distributed the property all around the county.

*

Mr Ivan Kernahan, a disabled ex-serviceman, con-tacted Oxfordshire District Council concerning some rubbish that he wanted removing from his farm. The Council, in a bid to prove their efficiency, sent a gang of workmen to clear the rubbish. The men walked past the pile of rubbish and took away the engine and gearbox that Mr Kernahan was waiting to install in his car.

*

A painting by Henri Matisse called *Le Bateau* was displayed for forty-seven days in New York's Museum of Modern Art hanging upside down, by mistake. Nobody realised.

★

In Ontario it was a sad day for the friends and relatives of Mrs Sadie Tuckey. She had been accidently knocked off her bicycle by a bus and killed. When the funeral was held, scores of mourners came to pay their last respects, but as the coffin was being carried to its final resting place the mourners themselves nearly died of shock when they saw the 'body' sit up in the coffin. Sadie was not dead at all! She had merely been stunned into a deep coma. The 'body' screamed, leapt out of the coffin with fright and ran off down the road, straight into the path of a bus – which killed her outright.

★

The BBC in London have one of the greatest libraries of recorded sound effects in the world and whatever the play or broadcast, an appropriate sound effect can be found, whether it is of a baby crying, a vase smashing, or the footsteps of an elephant tip-toeing through a swamp. Nothing is beyond them. So, when the King of Norway was going to broadcast to the nation, finding an official fanfare seemed no problem, except for the small fact that the Sound Effects Department read the order as 'funfair'! Instead of being introduced with bugles, the King was preceeded by a loud cry of: 'Roll up! Roll up! All the fun of the fair...' and a barrel organ playing *Over the Waves*.

★

A woman from Chichester was going to a very exclusive wedding and was prevented from entering the church by an usher.

'Excuse me', he said, 'are you a friend of the groom?'

'No', she replied, 'I'm the bride's mother.'

★

Special shelves were erected for a recent exhibition organised by the Royal Society for the Prevention of Accidents. Shortly after the exhibition opened, the shelves collapsed, injuring one of the visitors!

★

A couple from Manchester went off on holiday and had to put their dog in kennels for the two weeks they were away. On their return the husband dropped the wife off at their house so that she could unpack the suitcases and prepare a meal, and he drove on to collect their pet. He picked up the animal without any difficulty, but on the drive back it barked continually and no amount of talking, shouting, swearing, and loving care would calm it down.

'I can't think what's the matter with that dog', said the husband when he got back, 'I can't control him at all. Do you think he prefers it at the kennels?'

'Quite probably' said the wife. 'You've got the wrong dog!'

★

One cold autumnal Sunday, Mrs Dorothy Smith set off for church with her friend, just as they did every Sunday. The streets were unusually empty, but they put this down to the time of year and the particularly cold weather. On arriving at the church they were astonished to find that it was already packed to capacity and the only free seats were right at the very front. What's more, the congregation were already singing the first hymn. Red-faced and very conspicuous they made their way to the front pew as the hymn was finishing, and sat down with the rest of the congregation. The vicar then said the benediction.

Mrs. Smith had forgotten that the clocks had gone back an hour; they had arrived just in time for the *last* hymn.

★

In 1978, Mr James Callaghan, then British Prime Minister, was invited to open the new premises of the Anglo-Austrian Society and to unveil a plaque to commemorate the occasion. The photographers gathered around with cameras poised, waiting for the moment when the plaque was to be unveiled. As Mr Callaghan pulled the string, the plaque fell off the wall.

*

In Canada a mayor had to unveil a plaque, at City Hall in Prince George. The photographer who was reporting on the event decided to play a joke and so covered the plaque with a photograph of a naked female. He waited eagerly as the mayor unveiled the 'plaque' but he did so without even noticing the nude. When it was noticed, the photographer was sacked.

*

Things went slightly amiss in Vienna when authorities decided to build a special 'Women Only' wing at their police headquarters. This was originally to protect the susceptible young women from any intruding male police cadets, but the whole plan proved somewhat pointless when it was discovered that more than half the unmarried girls were already pregnant.

*

Policemen at Maidenhead, Berkshire, had very red faces when they went to free a prisoner they had locked in handcuffs. The key got stuck in the lock and they were unable to release it. The fire brigade had to be called in with cutting equipment before the man could be released.

*

Mrs Eileen Hargreaves of Richmond, Surrey, was giving a dinner party, and being noted for her pastry decided to serve her guests with some small individual apple pies that she had made a few months earlier and had stored in the deep freeze. She warmed the pies through gently, and the guests mouths began to water as they poured cream over the delicious-looking pies. The first mouthful resulted in ten surprised faces – the contents were steak and kidney.

*

An elderly New Yorker had been going deaf for a very long time and had worn a hearing aid for the best part of twenty-five years. On a routine visit to his local hospital it was discovered that the hearing aid had originally been put in the wrong ear. They changed it over and for the first time in a quarter of a century he could hear perfectly normally.

*

A Somerset man had been deaf since early childhood, until he visited a doctor for a check-up. It was then discovered that in his right ear was a small cork that he had put inside his ear as a child. The cork was removed and, at the age of 45, the man could hear again.

*